WHAT'S IN YOUR MOUTH?

From Defeat to Dominion: A Journey of Faith

INFLUENTIAL PRODUCTIONS
NAPLES, FLORIDA, U.S.A.

What's in Your Mouth?
From Defeat to Dominion: A Journey of Faith

Published by Influential Productions
Naples, Florida, U.S.A.

Editorial, design and production: Vision Book Producers, Naples, Florida: visionbookproducers.com
Front cover and bio portrait photography: Pure Fotografica, Naples, Florida: purefotografica.com

ISBN: 978-0-578-55780-9

I dedicate this book to my mom, Sarah Gardner, who taught and modeled the truths I've shared in this book. I've been so blessed to have a mother who fully lives out her faith in Christ. Through watching and listening to her, I grew to understand the absolute necessity of speaking God's promises when facing life's challenges or even to encourage and strengthen my soul. I have countless memories of watching her declare promise after promise that she had typed out on several pages of paper. I would not be the woman I am today, nor would I have achieved my God-given goals, without her continually pouring her unfailing love and wealth of experiential knowledge into me. I am eternally grateful. I love you, Mom!

ENDORSEMENT

I've known Pastor Tracy Boyd for years and she is not only a productive pastor, but a productive person as well. She's a woman of great character and prayer. I've watched her take an embryonic church and observed it grow to mega-church status. That's why, when I got a copy of *What's in Your Mouth?*, I read it—and with great interest. I was not disappointed, for this book generates the insight and revelation for your stepping into God's abundance in your life.

I'm a great believer in the power of your words, and Tracy has captured the essence of their potential to transform lives. Biblical and secular research alike reveals the efficacy of your words. One such vehicle is *psycholinguistics*: the study of how words affect your life. It has been discovered when you confess a thing it gets into your heart, or personal belief system (PBS), 10%. If you confess it with imagination (see it), it gets into your PBS 55%. If you confess things with imagination and emotion (feeling), it gets into your PBS or heart 100%. Words create thoughts, thoughts create feelings, and actions follow your emotion. Words are powerful tools when harnessed properly.

Today this must-read book has captured the various vehicles of how your words can take you from defeat to dominion, from struggle to victory. Tracy Boyd shows you how the words of your mouth affect your heart, and how you always manifest what's in your heart. She shows you how your words can create the presence of God in your life, and how they can affect your physical and emotional healing. Lastly, she shows how words can direct you to prosperity and abundance.

What you hold in your hand is a simple and practical guide to dominating your life rather than being dominated by life. Take this book, read it, do it, and watch victory and triumph characterize your life.

Ron McIntosh
President, Ron McIntosh Ministries
Author of books including *The Missing Ingredient*,
The Greatest Secret, and *Quest for Revival.*

A WORD FROM TRACY BOYD

Over the years I've often pondered why some followers of Christ seem to have God's blessing and favor on their lives while others struggle constantly in most every area. I'm talking about wonderful people who have a serving heart, read their Bibles, attend church regularly, and hear great faith-filled messages weekly.

When believers say, "Pastor Tracy, the Word of God isn't working in my life like it does in the lives of others," my first question is always, "What's in your mouth?" As odd as this question may sound, I ask it because, for some reason, these Christians do not fully know the purpose of why God created them, nor do they understand the powerful, creative element He gave them through the words of their mouths.

God made us in His own image and likeness when He created the world with the words He spoke. Likewise, we establish our lives with the words we speak, whether they are deliberate or unintentional.

Our words are power capsules. With our words we decree good or bad, life or death, blessing or cursing. With our words we set the spiritual tone in our homes, our businesses, and our churches. In essence, when we line up our mouths with what the Word of God says about us, we use our words as spiritual power tools to bring forth all that is in our hearts, to establish our futures, and to declare the very presence of God in our lives.

Some people may say, "Oh, but you don't understand, Pastor Tracy, that won't work for me because I have limitations in my life." Those limitations people list may include anything from "I come from a poor family" to "I don't have a college education" or "I've had this physical condition since I was born." Still others may say, "I've suffered terrible abuse in my life" or "I never seem to make the right decisions." When it comes to people's descriptions of their limitations and circumstances, I've heard it all. In fact, some of the issues people deal with, I've actually experienced in my own life.

The book you now hold in your hands relates my faith journey from defeat to dominion. In my story I convey how learning to use my words to change my circumstances opened the door to the life of blessing and favor I'm now living. But more than a story of my personal journey, this book will serve as a tool to help you move into the abundant life God has planned for you. Whether you're struggling to climb out of a pit of defeat or you just need to recalibrate the faith you're already walking in, you'll find in the pages to come the practical information you need to take charge of your life and change your circumstances through the words you speak.

The psalmist David said, *Bless the Lord, O my soul, and forget not all His benefits: Who satisfies your mouth with good things, so that your youth is renewed like the eagle's* (Psalms 103:2, 5 NKJV). Once you learn exactly *what* these good things are, you'll never again allow the words of your mouth to work against you.

I invite you to join me for a powerful and life-changing journey of discovery as we find the answers to the question *What's in your mouth?*

Terry Boyd

CONTENTS

CHAPTER ONE

YOUR FUTURE IS IN YOUR MOUTH

"Whoever ... believes that those things he says will be done, he will have whatever he says."

MARK 11:23 (NKJV)

I couldn't understand why, after taking multiple rounds of antibiotics, I was still battling the infection raging in my body.

I knew what the Bible said about healing. I believed Jesus had already provided healing for me, that by the stripes of Jesus I was healed. I had prayed for myself, and others had prayed for me, yet months had passed, and I just couldn't get free from the thing.

I was lying on my side, pondering and saying to myself a particular verse from the Bible the Lord had brought to my mind: *Then God blessed them, and God said to them, "Be fruitful and multiply; fill the earth and subdue it; have dominion over the fish of the sea, over the birds of the air, and over every living thing that moves on the earth"* (Genesis 1:28 NKJV).

Unsure what the account of creation had to do with my situation, I asked, "What are you trying to tell me, God?" That's when I began to sense His voice inside of me saying, "I've given you dominion over the earth. Subdue the earth. You're made in my image; subdue the earth. I've given you dominion, Tracy, so subdue the earth!" I still didn't understand what He meant by subduing the earth, but then, all of a sudden, it was as if a curtain opened and in my mind I was back in my high-school chemistry class.

I remembered our class had been studying the periodic table, the arrangement of chemical elements that can be used to derive relationships between various elemental properties. On that particular day the teacher had walked into the classroom carrying a bucket in each hand. One bucket had been filled with dirt, the other with water. He'd placed the buckets on his desk and said, "You each are a mixture of earth and water. This is what you are."

That's when it hit me: my physical body was made of 70 percent water, and the rest was *earth*. Now I understood what the Spirit of God was saying to me: my *body* was my earth. Again God said, "Tracy, subdue your earth. Take dominion over your earth. Command your earth to line up!"

I slid out of bed, stood to my feet, and declared, "In the name of Jesus, I command you, infection, leave my body!" Then I talked to my body and said, "Body, you're made of earth. Be healed. Be whole. I subdue you in the name of Jesus!" I'd never spoken that way before, but immediately I literally felt a change;

something was different in my body. I'd battled that infection for six months, yet in an instant it was gone.

That was the day I tapped into the understanding of how I could exercise dominion and authority through the words I spoke. My body—this "earth" that God said in the beginning mankind is to subdue—came under the authority of the words of my mouth.

Some may say, "Well, that worked for you, Tracy; you're a pastor. But what about me?" I certainly wasn't a pastor when I first learned to take authority, exercise dominion, and speak the Word of God. I was a young mother who believed the Bible and was determined to fulfill God's plan and purpose for my life. What I didn't yet realize was that I held my future in my mouth and could have whatever I said—as long as it aligned with the Word of God.

My journey of faith began with this verse from the New Testament: *By faith we understand that the worlds were framed by the word of God, so that the things which are seen were not made of things which are visible* (Hebrews 11:3 NKJV). The word *world* means "an unbroken age; a perpetuity of time; substance; eternity; vital force." The word *framed* means "to put together; to arrange; to mend." To paraphrase this verse, we could say that by faith (by believing and trusting), we understand that God put together substance by the words of His mouth.

In other words, when God spoke, the invisible realm became visible.

We see this truth established in the opening sentences of the

Bible. *In the beginning God created the heavens and the earth. Now the earth was formless and empty; darkness was over the surface of the deep, and the Spirit of God was hovering over the waters. And God said, "Let there be light," and there was light* (Genesis 1:1–3). Notice God didn't have to roll up His sleeves and create light with His hands. He merely said, *"Let there be light,"* and there was light. The invisible became visible when God spoke.

Imagine the words of your mouth being so powerful that they can alter the course of your life.

For many of us, our first exposure to the effect energy can have on matter was in a science class where we observed sound vibrations causing water to ripple. Imagine the level of energy coming forth from God's voice, so powerful that it created light. Now imagine the words of your mouth being so powerful that they can alter the course of your life. You may be thinking, *Wait a minute—I'm not God, so how can my words be that powerful?*

You're not God. However, you are His child and you are made in His image: *Then God said, "Let us make mankind in our image, in our likeness"* (Genesis 1:26). We oftentimes forget we are made in the image and likeness of God. While the words *image* and *likeness* may appear to be the same, they actually have two different meanings in the original language. *Image* means "resemblance," while *likeness* means "manner."

Knowing mankind was fashioned after God in both resemblance and manner, I can envision Adam taking his first walk in the garden and all creation thinking, *Oh, here comes God!* But then as Adam came closer, it was clear to see it was actually Adam and not God. That's how closely Adam's created image reflected God's resemblance and manner. If God's manner is to speak things into existence with His words, then our manner is to speak things into existence with our words.

GOD CREATED US WITH A PURPOSE

One of the things I like best about the book of Genesis is how it beautifully illustrates God's original intent for mankind.

Let's take a closer look at Genesis 1:28, the same verse God had me meditate on when I received my healing: *Then God blessed them, and God said to them, "Be fruitful and multiply; fill the earth and subdue it; have dominion over the fish of the sea, over the birds of the air, and over every living thing that moves on the earth"* (NKJV). Notice God *blessed* them, and the way He blessed them was with His words. He didn't just say *bless you* as we might do when someone sneezes. He actually declared a fivefold blessing over the man and woman: (1) *"Be fruitful,"* (2) *"multiply,"* (3) *"fill the earth,"* (4) *"subdue"* the earth, and (5) *"have dominion."*

God's original intent, or purpose, was that mankind have

dominion, which means "to tread down; subjugate; prevail against; reign; rule."

God had dominion over the heavens; that's what He ruled. Once He'd created mankind, He then made kids in His image who were to have dominion on earth, where He had already established a fertile environment designed to sustain the life forms He was about to bring forth. God had already created and blessed mankind; He was now ready to form the first human body. *Then the Lord God formed a man from the dust of the ground and breathed into his nostrils the breath of life, and the man became a living being* (Genesis 2:7).

God didn't form the first man, Adam, and leave him alone to fend for himself in an unfamiliar place. God developed Adam and trained him. Our heavenly Father was the original developer and trainer of mankind. God taught Adam how to use his words to take dominion, and here's how He did it: *Now the Lord God had formed out of the ground all the wild animals and all the birds in the sky. He brought them to the man to see what he would name them; and whatever the man called each living creature, that was its name* (Genesis 2:19).

God was teaching Adam about the power of his words. Within that training-ground environment, God was developing Adam to operate in like manner with Himself. Operating in His own image and likeness has always been God's plan for mankind. In the beginning He gave us the ability to subdue and have dominion through the words we speak, and that pattern has never changed. Jesus demonstrated that pattern over and over throughout His earthly ministry, as we see in this familiar story of Him teaching near the shore of a lake:

> That day when evening came, he said to his disciples, "Let us go over to the other side." Leaving the crowd behind, they took him along, just as he was, in the boat. There were also other boats with him. A furious squall came up, and the waves broke over the boat, so that it was nearly swamped. Jesus was in the stern, sleeping on a cushion. The disciples woke him and said to him, "Teacher, don't you care if we drown?"
>
> He got up, rebuked the wind and said to the waves, "Quiet! Be still!" Then the wind died down and it was completely calm (Mark 4:34–39).

Notice Jesus *talked* to the storm. He rebuked the wind and He *said,* "Quiet! Be still!" Jesus was operating in like manner to God, just as God had always intended. Jesus used His words to exercise dominion and authority.

Jesus didn't speak only to the weather; He also exercised dominion in front of His disciples when He spoke to a tree.

> The next day as they were leaving Bethany, Jesus was hungry. Seeing in the distance a fig tree in leaf, he went to find out if it had any fruit. When he reached it, he found nothing but leaves, because it was not the season for figs. Then he said to the tree, "May no one ever

> eat fruit from you again." And his disciples heard him say it.
>
> In the morning, as they went along, they saw the fig tree withered from the roots. Peter remembered and said to Jesus, "Rabbi, look! The fig tree you cursed has withered!"
>
> "Have faith in God," Jesus answered. "Truly I tell you, if anyone says to this mountain, 'Go, throw yourself into the sea,' and does not doubt in their heart but believes that what they say will happen, it will be done for them" (Mark 11:12–14, 22–23).

Jesus was saying to His disciples—and to you and me—that we can do what He does. When we have faith in God, we can speak to the mountains in our lives, those situations and circumstances that do not line up with the Word of God and His will. We can speak to illness, addiction, lack, or whatever we may be dealing with, and take the dominion that is already ours in Jesus Christ.

Jesus said, "If *anyone* says to this mountain." I used to think He was talking only to really holy and special people who never left their houses because they prayed all day. Special people like evangelists, pastors, prophets, and teachers. But that's not what Jesus said. He said a*nyone* who has faith in God and does not doubt in his or her heart can speak to a mountain and see it move.

THE POWER OF WORDS

Jesus said, "*The words I have spoken to you—they are full of Spirit and life*" (John 6:63). Even science now affirms what we know to be true about the power of words. Dr. Masaru Emoto is the author of several volumes of work titled *Messages from Water*, which detail his numerous experiments that monitored the molecular structure of water while he spoke words over it.

When he spoke loving words over a container of water, the result was the creation of beautiful crystal-like formations. When he spoke negative words, the crystals became deformed and broken. I watched a video experiment conducted by Dr. Emoto in which he placed rice into three glass beakers and then covered the rice with water. Every day for a month he said the words *thank you* to the first beaker and *you're an idiot* to the

All too often we say things without really thinking of the power of our words.

second beaker, and he completely ignored the third beaker. At the end of the month, the rice in the first beaker had fermented, giving off a strong, pleasant aroma. The rice in the second beaker had turned black, while the rice in the third beaker had rotted.

Knowing our bodies are made up of 70 percent water, we

need to ask ourselves these questions: What am I speaking over my body? More importantly, what is my body producing?

As I grew in my understanding of the power of my words, one of the books that made an impact on me was *The Fourth Dimension* by Dr. David Yonggi Cho, the South Korean pastor of the world's largest congregation. In his book Dr. Cho gives the account of his lunch meeting with a famous neurosurgeon who was sharing new findings about the power of speech. The neurosurgeon explained the newly discovered connection between speech and the central nervous system, which was supported by numerous experiments conducted over a long period of time. The doctor cited study examples of how people had consistently spoken something—whether good or bad—over their bodies for a period of time and how what they'd said had come to pass.

When Dr. Cho mentioned he already knew this principle, the neurosurgeon asked *how* he knew it since Cho was a pastor and not a doctor or scientist. Dr. Cho responded, "It's in the Bible," and then he quoted Proverbs 18:21: *Death and life are in the power of the tongue.*

I remember hearing the account of a particular man who had an exceptionally stressful job. Anytime the end of the workday came and his coworkers asked him about his plans for the evening, he'd say, "I just want to be brain dead." If friends asked him to go to dinner on a work night, he'd say, "No, I just want to go home and be brain dead." Of course, we understand the man meant he wanted to be alone and not have to think about his work; however, words are powerful.

One day as he was driving home, witnesses said he pulled his car to the side of the road and stopped. When he got out of the car, he stood for a moment and then fell to the ground. I don't know whether he may have had a stroke or an aneurysm, but he was taken to the hospital where he was declared "brain dead." He never regained consciousness. This man neither knew he held his future in his mouth, nor did he know the power of his words.

I heard of another man who used to say, "You know, my grandfather died of a heart attack at the age of fifty-nine, and my dad died of a heart attack at the same age. I'll probably die of a heart attack at age fifty-nine too." And that's exactly what happened to him.

The point I want to make is that all too often we say things without really thinking of the power of our words. I've heard believers say things like "I'm scared to death" or "I'm never going to get that job" or "My marriage isn't ever going to get better." In essence, what they're saying is, "I'm scared to death, I'm never going to get that job, my marriage isn't going to get better—and that's the way I want it to be!" This statement sounds ridiculous, but in reality it's exactly what we're saying when we agree with our circumstances instead of using our words to take dominion *over* the circumstances. The Bible addresses the importance of our taking control of what we say.

> Indeed we all make many mistakes. For if we could control our tongues, we would be perfect and could

> also control ourselves in every other way.
>
> We can make a large horse go wherever we want by means of a small bit in its mouth. And a small rudder makes a huge ship turn wherever the pilot chooses to go, even though the winds are strong. In the same way, the tongue is a small thing that makes grand speeches.
>
> But a tiny spark can set a great forest on fire. And among all the parts of the body, the tongue is a flame of fire. It is a whole world of wickedness, corrupting your entire body. It can set your whole life on fire (James 3:2–6 NLT).

I'm not saying we won't make mistakes and say things without considering the power of our words. When we slip, all we have to do is repent, which simply means to go in a different direction, and then say what God's Word says about our situation. For instance, if you say, "I'm scared to death," say instead, "For God has not given me a spirit of fear, but of power and of love and of a sound mind" or "In all things I am more than a conqueror" or "I can do all things through Christ" (see 2 Timothy 1:7; Romans 8:37; Philippians 4:13).

When you and I, as children of God who have the very Spirit of God living in us, actually speak God's Word out loud, we release His supernatural power into our lives.

GOD'S WORD IS ALIVE

Whether we enjoy reading the Word of God in a favorite Bible or on a device, what we see when we begin to read is a bunch of words. In reality those words are *alive*.

According to Hebrews 4:12, *the word of God is alive and active. Sharper than any double-edged sword, it penetrates even to dividing soul and spirit, joints and marrow; it judges the thoughts and attitudes of the heart.* Because the word is alive, it can do something powerful. What a dynamic truth about the Word of God. However, it brings up this question: what determines if the words in the Bible are alive? The answer is, the individual who is reading the Bible. In other words—we do!

> He's given us the ability to establish dominion through the words we speak.

God doesn't push Himself on anybody; rather, He cooperates with the free will He's given to each of us. When we mix our faith with the Word of God, believing God is speaking to us and His promises are personal to each of us, the Word becomes alive. Is it possible to read or hear the Word and not have it come alive? According to Hebrews 4:2 the answer is *yes*. *For indeed the gospel was preached to us as well as to them; but the word which they heard did not profit them, not being mixed with faith in those who heard it* (NKJV). Again, we are the ones who determine if God's Word comes alive in our hearts and lives. The Word comes alive when we mix it with our faith, when we *believe* that what God has said is true before we see any physical evidence.

I like the way the Bible describes its words as "active." They are not just words on a page; they are meant to *do something* in our lives. We can expect our words to accomplish God's will in our lives just as God expects His words to accomplish their purpose: *"As the rain and the snow come down from heaven, and do not return to it without watering the earth ... so is my word that goes out from my mouth: it will not return to me empty, but will accomplish what I desire and achieve the purpose for which I sent it"* (Isaiah 55:9–11).

This passage in Isaiah is a wonderful promise from God, but it is not a promise we will need in heaven. It's meant to do something for us here on earth. In His great mercy and love for us, God shows us how to conduct ourselves successfully in this life. He's given us the ability to establish dominion through the words we speak. Truly, we hold our very futures in our mouths.

The Word of God allows us to pull life from the invisible realm into the visible realm through our words. Jesus explained it like this: *"The Spirit gives life; the flesh counts for nothing. The words I have spoken to you—they are full of the Spirit and life"* (John 6:63). The word *life* in this verse means "gives life; quickens." In other words the Holy Spirit makes the words alive; He is doing something akin to what He did in the beginning when He brooded over the face of the deep. When God said, *"Let there be light,"* He spoke the future and immediately the Holy Spirit began to move. Likewise, when we declare our futures with our mouths, the Holy Spirit engages with the words we speak to bring them to pass.

Everything we see in the natural, physical world had its inception in the unseen, spiritual realm. Again, Jesus said, *"It is the Spirit who gives life"* (John 6:63 NKJV). The word *life* in the original language is *zoe,* which means "the God kind of life." *Zoe* is the full, abundant, prosperous, purpose-filled life God always intended us to have. In essence, Jesus was saying, "The words I'm speaking to you come from the invisible realm of the Spirit, and they will allow you to experience God's full, prosperous, and purpose-filled life."

As a pastor, I've seen how the words coming out of an individual's mouth have the power to change any situation. I remember one young girl who called me and said she was battling depression. She needed immediate help, so I told her about three particular worship songs I wanted her to listen to. She was familiar with all three, so I said, "Okay, here's what I want you to do: First, hang up the phone. I want you to listen to these three songs, and then I want you to worship God as you listen to them. Finally, I want you to begin to speak positive words over yourself—out loud."

About twenty minutes later she called to tell me the spirit of depression had broken. This happened because she took her place of authority and began to worship God. She established her dominion over depression by the words she spoke. That girl's future freedom was in her mouth, and when she decreed it, the Holy Spirit established it.

Simply put, we were created to lead our lives, not to have our lives lead us.

YOU CAN FRAME YOUR DESTINY

The process for building a home is pretty much the same whether one lives in a tiny house or a mansion (though most of us reside in dwellings that lie somewhere between the two in size). One of the most important steps in constructing a solid structure is framing. The frame is the skeleton of the house that gives it support, shape, and the ability to weather all kinds of exterior conditions.

Builders frame a house according to a set of blueprints prepared by an architect, the person whose job it is to design houses and make sure they are correctly constructed in accordance with his or her plan and purpose.

As believers, we often refer to God as "the architect of our lives," a concept supported by the Word. God said, *"Before I formed you in the womb I knew you, before you were born I set you apart"* (Jeremiah 1:5), and *"For I know the plans I have for you … plans to prosper you and not to harm you, plans to give you a hope and a future"* (Jeremiah 29:11).

If God is the architect of our lives, then we are the framers of our destinies. No two of us are exactly alike; we are each unique and special individuals, created by God with a plan and purpose. But it is up to each of us to frame our own destiny, and the way to do it is through the words we speak.

Sadly, many people believe the lie that says, "I'm a mistake. I was created by happenstance." Nothing could be further from the truth! You are not holding and reading this book by "happenstance"—you matter, and your life matters. When God created you, He did so with destiny in mind. You'll never be satisfied or content with your life until you walk in the destiny He has prepared for you.

You are God's masterpiece.

In today's world people lead busy lives. I believe the reason some people move so fast throughout their days is they don't want to answer the question, why am I alive? They may be moving, but in truth they are merely moving side to side. None of us can truly move forward until we understand we are made in the image and likeness of God, He formed us for a purpose, and we are to do something great for Him in this life. When we step into this truth, life becomes an adventure.

You are God's masterpiece. As such, you have the ability to shake a city—and literally change it—to help hurting people. God sees you as a person of destiny. Is that how you see yourself? If you don't like where you are, what you see, or what's going on around you, then you can frame your future by the words of your mouth.

I believe the Spirit of God is wooing you right now. He's saying, "I want to show you things you've never seen before; I want to show you what I see." Perhaps you've accepted as truth words others have spoken over you, words that have caused you to conform to the ways of this world. The world's words will always limit you because they never line up with God's Word. You can break the power of the world's words by first doing what the Bible says: *And do not be conformed to this world, but be transformed by the renewing of your mind, that you may prove what is that good and acceptable and perfect will of God* (Romans 12:2).

Next, choose to receive the peace Jesus has already provided for you. He said, "*Peace I leave with you; my peace I give to you. I do not give to you as the world gives. Do not let your hearts be troubled and do not be afraid*" (John 14:27).

There's a supernatural peace available to you as a child of God. All you have to do to experience this peace is to simply receive it and then frame it with the words of your mouth, saying, "I have the peace of God. God does not lie; therefore, I *have* His peace!" Choosing to frame your life with God's words pulls that which is in the invisible realm into the visible realm.

I want to challenge you to examine your life right now and ask yourself this question: am I living the life God has planned for me? If you are not walking in the fullness of all God has provided for you in Jesus Christ, begin to speak God's Word and wisdom over your life and situation.

You may say, "But, Pastor Tracy, where do I start?" The Bible says, *If you need wisdom, ask our generous God, and he will give it to you. He will not rebuke you for asking* (James 1:5). The Bible is full of scriptures you can use to renew your mind and also declare out loud to frame your destiny.

If you are sick, you can do as I did and subdue your body, commanding it to be healed and whole. You can declare, "By the stripes of Jesus, I am healed!" (see Isaiah 53:5; 1 Peter 2:24).

If you are dealing with fear, you can declare, "I will fear no evil for You are with me," or "No weapon formed against me will prosper" (see Psalms 23:4; Isaiah 54:17).

If you have a material need or are suffering any kind of lack, you can declare, "God supplies all of my need according to His riches in glory by Christ Jesus" (see Philippians 4:19).

If you have concerns for your children, you can declare, "All of my children shall be taught of the Lord, and they will have great peace" (see Isaiah 54:13).

If you're facing a decision and don't know what to do, you can declare, "In all my ways I will acknowledge God, and He will direct my path" (see Proverbs 3:6).

Whether you are a new Christian or a seasoned believer, the biblical truths and principles outlined in this book have the ability to impact your life in a powerful, dynamic way. But the choice is yours: you can speak death or you can speak life. God said, *"I have set before you life and death, blessings and curses. Now choose life, so that you and your children may live"*(Deuteronomy 30:19).

Your future is in your mouth.

DISCUSSION QUESTIONS

How does the account of creation demonstrate that we can cause the invisible realm to become visible in our lives? (See Genesis 1:1–3.)

How did God teach Adam to use his words to take dominion in the earth? (See Genesis 2:19.)

How do we cause God's Word to come alive in our hearts? (See Hebrews 4:2.)

How can we break the power of negative words that have established limitations in our lives? (See Romans 12:2; John 14:27.)

Is there a circumstance in your life, good or bad, that is a result of words you have spoken?

When God told Adam to subdue the earth (see Genesis 1:28), *what did the "earth" include?*

How did Jesus exercise authority?

CHAPTER TWO

YOUR HEART IS IN YOUR MOUTH

Above all else, guard your heart, for everything you do flows from it.

PROVERBS 4:23

I was beyond happy when I learned I was pregnant with my first child. My thoughts were constantly on my baby: *Will I have a boy or girl? Will he or she look like me or like my husband? What color should I paint the nursery?*

I enjoyed dreaming about the precious life I was about to bring into the world, but from a practical standpoint I knew I needed to do something to prepare for my time of delivery. That "something" meant dealing with two specific fears that had become strongholds in my mind: fear of miscarriage and fear of the pain of delivery. Several of my friends had experienced recent miscarriages, and I feared the same thing might happen to me. As for my fear of pain, well, I'd watched enough movies to know childbirth was no picnic in the park.

I discovered an amazing book by Jackie Mize titled *Supernatural Childbirth.* The subtitle was *Experiencing the Promises of God Concerning Conception and Childbirth.* The book was an account of the author's physical inability to have children and how—when she learned to meditate on God's Word and believe His promises—she subsequently gave birth to four children.

I virtually devoured that book. When I finished reading the final page, I closed the cover and declared, "I'm going to have a supernatural, pain-free childbirth!"

Upon arriving at the hospital months later to deliver my child,

Whatever comes out of the mouth has its origin in the heart.

I was ready to experience my own supernatural childbirth. But that is *not* what happened. There was nothing pain free about the back labor that felt to me as if my back were breaking with each contraction. I was a mess, and I remember begging the nurse, "Do something—now!"

It's said that a woman forgets the pain of delivery once she holds her child in her arms. That was certainly not true for me. I had read *Supernatural Childbirth.* I *knew* the promises of God in that book, yet my experience had been nothing like the supernatural childbirth experience I'd expected.

I didn't realize it at the time, but there's a big difference in having *knowledge* of God's Word and actually having God's Word *hidden in your heart* as the psalmist had when he said, *I have hidden your word in my heart* (Psalms 119:11). After reading Jackie Mize's book, I had the knowledge of God's promises in my head; however, they weren't in my heart. There is quite a difference between what is in your heart and what is in your head.

Jesus said, *"For the mouth speaks what the heart is full of"* (Luke 6:45). The New Living Translation says it this way: *"What you say flows from what is in your heart,"* and the New King James Version says, *"For out of the abundance of the heart [the] mouth speaks."* In other words, whatever comes out of the mouth has its origin in the heart. What is lodged in the heart is a big deal. This is why Proverbs 4:23 says, *Above all else, guard your heart, for everything you do flows from it.* Notice this verse begins with the phrase *above all else*, which indicates the very next words are important and we're to make them a priority: we are to *guard our hearts*. The question then becomes, guard them against what?

I believe we are to guard our hearts against *anything* contrary to God's character, His ways, and His design for our lives, all of which are scripted on the pages of His Word. The problem is that our hearts have *already been shaped* by the environments we were raised in and are currently living in—most of which are negative.

When the Word of God talks about *the heart of man* it is not referring to the natural, physical heart. Rather, it is speaking of the heart of our inner man (the seat of our thoughts, feelings, and intellect). To better understand the inner heart and how it functions, I've created the following diagram that depicts the two sides of the heart.

On one side of the heart is the spirit; on the other side is the soul. The spirit is the place where God's Spirit comes to live permanently. This spirit side is where the miracle of being born anew takes place, where we become children of God. When someone yields his or her heart to God, God's Spirit comes into that person's spirit. The spirit side is supernaturally and instantaneously transformed. This new birth is a free gift. The person's soul, which is made up of the mind, will, and emotions, is not transformed instantaneously but through a process.

Now let me explain what I mean by the heart already being negatively shaped by environments. Think of the heart as a computer that can accept any kind of data. We've all taken a numerous data into our hearts, data, which in turn have influenced and shaped our belief systems. When I refer to our "belief systems," I mean those ideas we believe true of ourselves and others.

I created the acronym OATs to identify three particular

natural influences that can access our hearts. These influences are observations, associations, and teachings.

Observations have to do with anything we see and fix our attention on, including photographs, written materials, and information from TV, movies, or the Internet.

Associations involve our relationships with others, including the experiences connected to those relationships. Some of these relationships may have been positive, others negative or abusive.

Teachings are the doctrines, precepts, and practical training we received from teachers, professors, authority figures, even celebrities.

It's really important to note that many of these OATs are directly influenced by Satan. First John 5:19 says, *We know that we are children of God, and that the whole world is under the control of the evil one.* These OATs enter our hearts through our senses; they influence the mind, will, and emotions, and finally come out of our mouths as shown in the diagram below. It's a cycle we are not aware is happening.

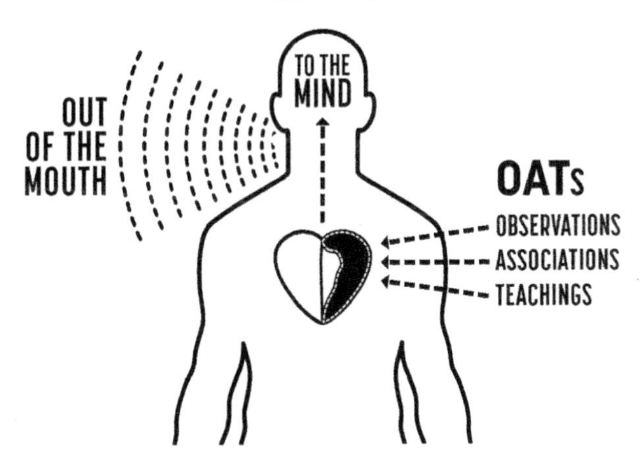

Consider the words *I can't.* Most people respond with "I can't" when asked to do something they've never done before, such as playing a particular sport, solving a problem, or overcoming a difficult situation. The reason people think they can't do such things is that, at some point, they were probably told they weren't good at sports, they weren't smart, or they'd never succeed. They stored these ideas in their hearts as truths that eventually came out of their mouths in the form of "I can't."

So how can we change an "I can't" mentality to an "I can" mentality? By changing the origin of what's coming out of our mouths. In other words, by changing what's in our hearts. If world-influenced OATs shape a heart to be negative and limited, God-honoring OATs can transform a heart to be positive and limitless.

Proverbs 4:20–23 says, *My son, pay* attention *to what I say; turn your* ear *to my words. Do not let them out of your* sight, *keep them within your heart; for they are life to those who find them and health to one's whole body. Above all else, guard your heart, for everything you do flows from it* (emphasis added).

Notice how this scripture reveals the entry points to the heart: what we give our *attention* to affects our feelings; through our *ears* we hear; through our *eyes* we see. So the first thing in transforming a heart is being intentional about having God-honoring OATs in our lives.

The second, and most important, thing we need to be intentional about is the changing of our thoughts. Scripture again reveals something about our human nature: *For as [a man] thinks in his heart, so is he* (Proverbs 23:7 NKJV). Whatever we think makes its way to our mouths, and it's again shaping our lives. Our minds need be transformed.

The Bible says, *Do not conform to the pattern of this world, but be transformed by the renewing of your mind* (Romans 12:2). The word *transformed* in the Greek is *metamorphoō*. It's where

Meditating the Word is directly related to a supernatural, abundant, successful life.

we get the word *metamorphosis*, which describes the transformation of a caterpillar into a butterfly. Though none of us can see what is happening in the cocoon, once the creature emerges, we can all see that the caterpillar was transformed into something better. No longer crawling, it is now spreading its beautiful wings and flying.

The Word of God has power to renew, or change, thoughts. Our thoughts that have been changed begin to transform our lives. God desires to transform us from crawling in life—barely getting by, taking whatever comes our way—to winning in life. When we *intentionally* put God's Word in our hearts, our minds are renewed and we can then *choose* to say what God says about us. This process doesn't happen because we merely think about doing it; we have to train ourselves to do it.

The process of renewing the mind can be summarized with

one word: meditation. Biblical meditation is drastically different from the world's definition of meditation. Biblical meditation involves taking a truth, principle, or promise from the Word of God and *saying* it out loud over and over, as well as pondering, imagining, and emotionally experiencing that word. In other words, we are *saying, seeing,* and *feeling*; we are *engaging our senses.* When we hear ourselves say the Word, it produces a mountain-moving faith (see Romans 10:17). Meditating on the Word of God connects us to His design and removes any incorrect limitations we've established in our lives.

The Bible repeatedly affirms that meditating the Word is directly related to a supernatural, abundant, successful life. In Joshua 1:8 we see God handing Israel's baton of leadership from Moses to Joshua. God gave Joshua a mountainous plan to lead the under-qualified Israelites to conquer a vast land filled with fortified cities, experienced warriors, and giants. God instructed him to meditate in the Word of God and encouraged Joshua that, in doing so, he would have great success. Joshua was afraid, but God knew meditating the Word would change the limitations of fear in Joshua's heart to a fearless confidence.

God desires that we live supernatural, abundant, successful lives. He knows we live in a fallen world where we are bombarded with all kinds of negative influences that have the ability to bring us down. He provides the roadmap (the process) through meditating His Word—saying, seeing, and feeling the Word—to get us back to the original life He intended. The Word of God contains the truths, or belief systems, we get to live by.

I'm going to illustrate this process through the backdrop of a man named Abraham, whose story is detailed in the book of Genesis. God gave Abraham a promise that eventually Abraham believed.

ABRAHAM: THE FATHER OF FAITH

We often refer to Abraham as the "father of faith" because of the numerous ways he demonstrated his faith in God through his obedience to God's instructions.

Abraham was known as Abram when he first met the Lord. *The Lord said to Abram, "Go from your country, your people and your father's household to the land I will show you. I will make you a great nation, and I will bless you; I will make your name great, and you will be a blessing. I will bless those who bless you, and whoever curses you I will curse; and all peoples on earth will be blessed through you"* (Genesis 12:1–4). What amazing promises! I think any one of us would love to have tremendous blessings in our lives, our name be great, and the opportunity to be a blessing.

But oh the risks Abram had to take.

Abram didn't live like we do today. When we travel, we have the benefit of well-constructed, safe highways patrolled by local and state law enforcement. We have access to comfortable rest stops, food, and fuel along the way. In Abram's day people traveled in camel caravans for safety. Abram didn't have a GPS device, but then he couldn't have used one because he didn't know where God was taking him. It was just Abram, his wife, Sarai, and his nephew Lot who set out in faith—believing what God had said to Abram—for a land God promised to show him.

Notice God said to Abram, *"I will make you a great nation"* (Genesis 12:2). This statement undoubtedly caught Abram's attention for two reasons. First, he was seventy-five years old at the time; second, he and Sarai were childless. Back then anyone who was childless was considered cursed. God was offering Abram a great deal—blessings, honor, prestige, and children—if only he would trust and obey God.

At one time or another, we've all grappled with a promise God has given us.

God indeed blessed Abram as He'd promised. The Bible says, *Abram had become very wealthy in livestock and in silver and gold* (Genesis 13:2). But still there was no baby, no son who would eventually become a great nation. Abram struggled with believing the promise, obviously because it seemed so impossible. God, who is so gracious, helped Abram believe by engaging his *imagination.*

God said to Abram, *"Look around from where you are, to the north and south, to the east and west. All the land that you see I will give to you and your offspring forever. I will make your offspring like the dust of the earth, so that if anyone could count the dust, then your offspring could be counted. Go, walk through the length and breadth of the land, for I am giving it to you"* (Genesis 13:14–17).

God instructed Abram to look around. He was engaging Abram's "eye gate" to establish His promise in Abram's heart. When God described Abram's offspring as the dust of the earth by count, He was painting a mental picture for Abram, who was still childless. God wanted Abram to *see* the promise, not focus on his own limitations. Abram continued to walk with God and prosper, but still no baby. So again God engaged Abram's imagination and made a covenant with him:

> The Lord came to Abram in a vision: "Do not be afraid, Abram. I am your shield, your very great reward."
>
> But Abram said, "Sovereign Lord, what can you give me since I remain childless and the one who will inherit my estate is Eliezer of Damascus?" And Abram said, "You have given me no children; so a servant in my household will be my heir."
>
> Then the word of the Lord came to him: "This man will not be your heir, but a son who is your own flesh and blood will be your heir." He took him outside and said, "Look up at the sky and count the stars—if indeed you can count them." Then he said to him, "So shall your offspring be."
>
> Abram believed the Lord, and he credited it to him as righteousness (Genesis 15:1–6).

What got my attention in this passage were God's words, *"Do not be afraid."* He wouldn't have said that to Abram unless he had been afraid. Abram was grappling with the promise God had made about children; it was a promise that had not yet come to pass.

At one time or another, we've all grappled with a promise God has given us. When the promise doesn't come to pass in the timeframe we think it should, we begin to doubt; we begin to question our faith and the veracity of God's Word. I love the humanity of the Word of God in this passage. God understands mankind is oftentimes confronted with doubt, as Abram was and as we are. That's why He said, "Don't be afraid Abram, your reward is going to be great."

Abram pointed out to God that because he and Sarai remained childless, a servant would inherit his estate. In essence Abram was venting to God, which is something God will never rebuke us for doing. God listened, and then He reassured Abram, saying, "A son who is your own flesh will be your heir." And then to further paint a picture of the promise for Abram, God told him to *look up* at the stars. I can imagine Abram looking at those stars and seeing the faces of children, seeing their freckles, their smiles, and their tears.

The passage concludes by saying Abraham *believed* God, and God credited Abraham's faith as righteousness.

At the beginning of this story we saw a fearful Abram who was focused on his natural limitations rather than the promise of God. He saw himself as childless; he saw the impossibility of his situation. But God saw something completely different: He saw Abram as the father of multitudes of offspring.

At the age of ninety-nine, Abram was still childless. God appeared to Abram and again declared His audacious promise to make Abram a father of many nations, saying that kings would come from him. God then gave both Sarai and Abram something else to do to help them believe; God changed their names! He told Abram to change his name from Abram to Abraham, which means "father of a multitude," and Sarai to Sarah, which means "princess of a multitude." God wanted them to say and see what God Himself believed! We see in the Word that both Abraham and Sarah, on separate occasions, laughed at the idea of having a child at ages ninety-nine and eighty-nine. What was God going to do? Create new organs? God's response was, *"Is anything too hard for the Lord? I will return about this time next year, and Sarah will have a son"* (Genesis 18:14 NLT).

We all know it takes nine months to have a baby, yet the Lord said He would return in a *year* and Sarah would have a son. I personally think the purpose of the first three months of that year was to get Abraham and Sarah accustomed to their new names and the meaning of those names. Think about this: When Abraham wanted his dinner, he was actually saying to Sarah, "Princess of a multitude, I'm hungry." And when she answered Abraham, she was in reality saying, "Father of a multitude, let's eat!"

I can imagine their servants and all the people around them watching and not understanding what was going on as this really old couple bantered back and forth with each other. Perhaps the people thought something had happened to the old couple's minds; however, Abraham and Sarah were seeing what God saw and speaking what God had spoken. The words Abraham and Sarah spoke changed what was in their hearts, and, just as God had promised, a year later Sarah gave birth to a son, Isaac.

Abraham and Sarah had in their hearts limitations, which—if not removed—would have prevented them from receiving God's promise. Like Abraham and Sarah, we too have limitations that have entered our hearts through OATs: observations, associations, and teachings. Just as *seeing* what God had seen and *saying* what God had said caused faith to grow in Abraham and Sarah, so we too can grow in faith by choosing to *see* and *say* in accordance with God's promises and plans for our lives.

REMOVE THE LIMITATIONS

When I became pregnant with my second baby, I knew I needed to remove the limitations in my life; I needed to get rid of my fears of both miscarriage and painful childbirth—once and for all—so that I could bring another beautiful child into this world.

I turned again to Jackie Mize's book *Supernatural Childbirth*, but this time I read it four times and with a fresh perspective. I realized the author hadn't merely believed the promises of God and then waited for them to come to pass; she had spoken them and imagined them. She'd involved her senses and her emotions.

She hadn't simply *believed* the promises of God in her head; she'd *meditated* on them until they became entrenched in her heart.

I understood that I too had to get God's promises into my heart, so I began to write out scripture verses that meant something to me. I *saw* them and then I *said* them, involving my

> Faith is the spiritual substance that moves things from the unseen spiritual realm into the natural world.

senses and emotions in the process of meditating the Word of God. In the morning I would take time to *say* those verses out loud so that I could hear them and allow the Word of God to build my faith. I would *see* my muscles contracting without pain during my delivery. I actually got a detailed diagram of my reproductive organs and muscles so that I could accurately envision them. I was determined not to repeat my first childbirth experience. The Bible says, *Surely he took up our pain and bore our suffering* (Isaiah 53:4); therefore, if Jesus had already borne my pain, then I didn't need to bear it!

I'd lie in bed at night and see myself in the delivery room, my muscles contracting without pain. Then, without disturbing my husband sleeping beside me, I'd speak the promises of God over my body as I touched my muscles, commanding them to contract without pain. I did this faithfully every morning and night for the six months preceding the delivery of our baby.

Late in my pregnancy I woke up early one morning with an odd physical sensation that I can describe only as a steady rising and falling. I wasn't in any pain, so I lay quietly in bed, meditating the Word of God until it hit me: *I think these are contractions*. When I timed the rhythm of the sensations, I was surprised to learn they were four minutes apart.

"Wake up," I said as I shook my husband, "We have to go to the hospital; I'm having a baby!"

I was already dilated four centimeters when we arrived at the hospital, but I wasn't experiencing any discomfort. My labor moved quickly and without pain while we told jokes, laughed, and even ordered a pizza. When I was ready to deliver my daughter, I pushed twice, and there she was.

I had just experienced my first supernatural childbirth.

The difference between my two childbirth experiences was significant. The first time I read *Supernatural Childbirth*, I'd simply closed the book and walked away without dealing with my limitations. I'd not dealt with my fear of miscarriage and fear of pain by taking God's promises and speaking them until they took up residence in my heart. But when I took authority over my body, which is made up of 70 percent water and a bunch of dirt, my physical "earth" lined up with the Word of God and delivered my baby without pain or complication.

Why is it so important that we speak the Word of God? We find the answer to this question in Romans 10:17: *So then faith comes by hearing, and hearing by the word of God* (NKJV).

Notice faith comes by hearing and hearing, not just once or twice, but as the mouth continually speaks the Word of God. Why is faith so important in the life of a believer? Faith is the spiritual substance that moves things from the unseen spiritual realm into the natural world: *Now faith is the substance of things hoped for, the evidence of things not seen* (Hebrews 11:1 NKJV).

We engage our faith with our words. Jesus said, *"Truly I tell you, if anyone says to this mountain, 'Go, throw yourself into the sea' and does not doubt in their heart but believes that what they say will happen, it will be done for them"*(Mark 11:23). Jesus didn't say we are to think about the mountain or strategize about the mountain; we are to *speak* to it! He also said we are not to doubt in our hearts, which is the place where limitation resides.

I remember a powerful healing testimony from many years ago, before most everyone had ready access to advanced medical treatments and hospitals. A man with a terminal illness was receiving treatment from a doctor who not only believed in healing but also housed her terminal patients in her home. The doctor gave this man one verse of scripture and instructed him to meditate on it: *Christ redeemed us from the curse of the law by becoming a curse for us* (Galatians 3:13).

The bedridden man began to meditate this verse, saying, "Christ has redeemed me from the curse of the law. I am not cursed; I'm blessed and I'm healed." When he first started meditating the Word of God, he thought, *This is ridiculous; I'm dying.* A week went by, and he was still alive, meditating Galatians 3:13 as he lay in his bed. Another week went by, and then one day the doctor heard footsteps running around in one of her upstairs rooms where she housed her patients. She went to the foot of the staircase, and when she looked up, she saw the man standing there.

We can remove our limitations by changing what's in our hearts.

He said, "Doctor, do you know that Christ redeemed me from the curse of the law and I'm blessed?" He was completely healed. Meditating the Word of God had driven out the limitation of death that had been in his heart. Truly, this man's heart was in his mouth.

The Bible says, *It is written: "I believed; therefore I have spoken." Since we have that same spirit of faith, we also believe and therefore speak* (2 Corinthians 4:13). In modern vernacular we might say, "I believe what God says in His Word, so I'm going to say what He says. I'm not going to say what my situation looks like; I'm not going to say what the doctor's report says; I'm not going to say what my checkbook says; I'm not going to say what my marriage looks like—I'm only going to say what God says about me! I believe what God says about me. His Word is hidden in my heart; therefore, I will speak it."

We can remove our limitations by changing what's in our hearts through our seeing, speaking, and meditating the Word of God. We can't do this only one time and expect circumstances to change; I learned this fact the hard way with my first childbirth experience. The key to removing limitations and changing our circumstances through our words is *consistency.* Saying what God says on a consistent basis—day by day and week by week—is what changes the human heart.

Perhaps you have a promise from God that has not yet come to pass. You believe the Word of God and you are speaking His promise, but you've grown tired and you're questioning God just as Abraham did. I want to encourage you to persevere. Keep saying what God says until the situation changes and your promise comes to pass, knowing that *God's love has been poured out into [your heart] through the Holy Spirit, who has been given to [you]* (Romans 5:5).

This love that God has poured into your heart will never fail you. The Bible says, *Love is patient, love is kind. It does not envy, it does not boast, it is not proud. It does not dishonor others, it is not self-seeking, it is not easily angered, it keeps no record of wrongs. Love does not delight in evil but rejoices with the truth. It always protects, always trusts, always hopes, always perseveres. Love never fails* (1 Corinthians 13:4–8).

Guard your heart; protect and nourish it. Sow God's Word into your heart, and then speak forth the abundance that is there—because everything you do flows from your heart.

DISCUSSION QUESTIONS

How can we change an "I can't" mentality to an "I can" mentality? (See Proverbs 4:20–23.)

How did God engage Abram's imagination to support his faith in the promise of God? (See Genesis 13:14–17.)

When we are standing in faith for one of God's promises to come to pass in our lives, why is it important that we speak words of faith? (See Hebrews 11:1.)

The Bible says that as a man thinks in his heart, so is he. What does this mean? (See Proverbs 23:7).

Why is it important that we guard our hearts? (See Proverbs 4:23.)

What was the main change Abraham made that brought about the miracle of fathering a baby at age 100?

CHAPTER THREE

POWER IS IN YOUR MOUTH

"You will also declare a thing
and it will be established for you."

JOB 22:28 (NKJV)

At the beginning of each year my husband, James, and I make a list of things we want to see God do in our church, our family, and our businesses. The Bible says *nothing* is too hard for God, so when we make our list, we make sure our goals are big and audacious. In other words, if God doesn't show up, those goals won't happen.

In January 2017 our main goal for the church we pastor in Naples, Florida, was to have a debt-free building. We found specific promises in the Word that supported our faith. One such promise was Deuteronomy 28:12, *The Lord will open the heavens, the storehouse of his bounty, to send rain on your land in season and to bless all the work of your hands. You will lend to many nations but will borrow from none.* Another promise was Romans

13:8: *Owe no one anything except to love one another* (NKJV).

James and I actively engaged our faith with these promises we found in the Bible, meditating on them and declaring them out loud each and every day. But then in March we became aware of another problem. The church was expanding at a rapid rate; it wouldn't be long before the near filled-to-capacity building could no longer accommodate our vibrant, healthy, growing congregation. What good would a debt-free building do us if it couldn't accommodate our church family?

We sought God's wisdom and direction, which came to us in an unusual way in mid-2017. Someone approached us about another local church that was dealing with its own issues. Their building was much too large for their congregation, and they were wrestling with their debt. The individual who approached us knew we'd helped other struggling churches and asked if we would consider helping this one.

One day James and I decided we'd drive to the church so that we could locate it and look around. As it turned out, the pastor was there that day, so we had an impromptu meeting with him in his office. We listened as he told us about his congregation and their current need, and then James looked at him and said the most ridiculous thing: "Would you be open to a church swap?"

I certainly didn't see the question coming, and I'm sure that pastor didn't either. My initial thought was, *We're going to get thrown out of here right now,* but it didn't happen. Instead, that initial meeting was the catalyst for a series of subsequent meetings with church leaders and board members of both congregations.

Everyone agreed the church-swap deal was doable and we should move forward; however, it presented James and me with another problem. We were believing to be debt free by the end of 2017, and a church swap would *double* the existing debt.

Even so, we had peace about proceeding with the deal. So we kept God's Word in our hearts and in our mouths, and we continued to declare, "We are debt free!" as we moved forward with plans for the church swap.

Prayer is the means by which we establish and release the will of God.

A few months later a man contacted us and said he and his wife might be able to help us get into the new building, so we made an appointment to meet them at a local coffee shop. When the couple arrived, the first thing the man said was, "When I contacted you, we felt God was directing us to give you $100,000 to help with the new facility. But we've reconsidered, and we don't think that's what we're supposed to do."

James and I both stiffened as I thought, *That's not God—you're supposed to help us!*

The next thing out of the man's mouth was, "My wife and I have talked, and we feel God has confirmed we are to do the deal."

What? I wasn't sure if I knew what "do the deal" meant, but it sounded as if they wanted to take care of the entire debt. The couple confirmed that was what they wanted to do—and that is exactly what they did. Their gift of $3.5 *million* dollars enabled us to facilitate the church swap *and* be completely debt free in December 2017.

The Bible says that God *is able to do immeasurably more than all we ask or imagine, according to his power that is at work with us* (Ephesians 3:20). That power comes first through prayer and is then expressed through the words we speak.

Experience has taught me that nothing in this life happens without prayer, without having a relational conversation with God. As human beings we are designed to be relational, to commune and converse with others. When we converse with another person, an exchange takes place. Whether we share our thoughts, ideas, information, or feelings, something happens as a result of our conversation.

We are made in the image of God; therefore, we can conclude that He is the original relational being and that He desires to be in relationship with us. When we converse with God, an exchange takes place. We give Him all of our cares, and He gives us His wisdom, power, and love so that we are edified when we leave His presence.

Another aspect of prayer not talked about in many Christian circles (though Jesus consistently modeled it throughout His ministry) is that prayer is the means by which we establish and release the will of God in our personal lives and in the earth. In other words, prayer releases power.

After His disciples asked Jesus to teach them to pray, He

answered, "*When you pray, say: Our Father in heaven, hallowed be Your name. Your kingdom come. Your will be done on earth as it is in heaven*" (Luke 11:2 NKJV). When Jesus said, "Your kingdom come," He was referring to the domain of the king. When He said, "Your will be done on earth as it is in heaven," Jesus revealed the heart of the Father. He showed those with Him that God desires that the fullness of heaven—the peace, provision, healing, and comfort found there—be established on earth as well.

God wants each of us to experience this fullness in our lives, our families, our homes, and our cities; however, it is our responsibility to pray forth His will, saying, "Your kingdom come. Your will be done on earth as it is in heaven."

We know it is not God's will that anyone perish (see 2 Peter 3:9), but that all might come to the saving knowledge of Jesus Christ. Romans 10:9 says, *If you declare with your mouth, "Jesus is Lord," and believe in your heart that God raised him from the dead, you will be saved.* The word *saved* means "to preserve; to heal; to deliver; to protect; to do well; to be whole." The word *saved* is actually a reflection of God's intent for how we live our lives. Interestingly, the actual name of Jesus is derived from the Hebrew name *Joshua*, which means "salvation."

It is God's will that we experience now, in this lifetime on earth, all that comes with our salvation. When we get to heaven, we won't need healing, deliverance, or wholeness because we won't encounter any enemy resistance there; we will be with Jesus all the time. Everything that comes to us through salvation is to enable us to function on planet Earth in a wildly successful way. Jesus gave His life so that we can experience His kind of life. This is why it's important we study the life of Jesus, that we learn what He did and how He operated. Three years of His life were recorded so that you and I could see how to live and operate on the earth. His life is a picture of what's available to you and me.

OUR WORDS RELEASE GOD'S DOMINION

Following His resurrection, Jesus told His followers, *"All authority in heaven and on earth has been given to me. Therefore go and make disciples … teaching them to obey everything I have commanded you"* (Matthew 28:18). Jesus has given us the same authority that He operated in, and it is through prayer that we are allowed to exercise this authority.

One of my favorite verses is 1 John 4:17: *As He is, so are we in this world* (NKJV). God's plan is that you and I represent who He is to a world that's really hurting and that we release His dominion through the power of prayer. We learned in part 1 of this book that God's original intent for mankind was that we take dominion on earth: *Then God said, "Let Us make man in Our image, according to Our likeness; let them have dominion … over all the earth and over every creeping thing that creeps on the earth* (Genesis 1:26 NKJV).

How do we take this dominion? It's by our mouths that we release God's dominion in our lives. Some may wonder why we need to do such a thing. The answer is simple: there is a very real demonic realm that actively fights against the dominion of God being established throughout earth. The Bible says, *For our struggle is not against flesh and blood, but against rulers, against authorities, against the powers of this dark world and against the spiritual forces of evil in the heavenly realms* (Ephesians 6:12).

Through the power of prayer we actually release the will of God and hold at bay the will of the devil.

Our battle is not against our brothers, our sisters, our coworkers, or members of a political party. Our battle is against the evil rulers of the unseen world; this is where the battle is going on against anything from God coming to pass in our lives. Through the power of prayer we actually release the will of God and hold at bay the will of the devil.

Jesus is our model for prayer. Some may say, "Wait a minute, Pastor Tracy, Jesus was different from us. He was the Son of God." True. However, Jesus operated as a human being on the earth: *he made himself nothing by taking the very nature of a servant, being made in human likeness* (Philippians 2:7). In other words, Jesus stripped Himself of His divinity and took on flesh and blood. Jesus operated on earth the way Adam operated before he sinned. The Bible describes Jesus as the second, or last, Adam: *So it is written: "The first man Adam became a living being"; the last Adam, a life-giving spirit* (1 Corinthians 15:45).

Jesus operated as a human being, and He prayed as a human being. There were times when He fellowshipped with God in prayer, getting direction, comfort, and receiving a transfer of strength. There were times when He interceded for His friends and the people around Him. But then there were times when He boldly spoke forth the Word of God or the will of God, which are interchangeable, into a situation. This "speaking forth" is also a form of prayer—powerful prayer.

Whether we're fellowshipping with God, interceding for others, or speaking forth God's will into the earth, prayer is power in our mouths. It's the act of establishing dominion on earth. God has designed us to live amazing, victorious lives that reflect who Jesus is and all that that is ours through His sacrifice on the cross. While this life of health and wholeness is already ours, we are to access it and release it through prayer.

It is also our job to enforce what we've been given. This truth makes me think about something that happened at the end of WWII. Hitler's Nazis had lost the war, yet there was still a host of them occupying France. The American troops did not leave Paris immediately; instead, they stayed to enforce the victory. Likewise, though we've been given much, we still have to *enforce* the victory Jesus won for us.

It saddens me to see people who are missing out on all God has prepared for them. Instead of leading their lives, their lives and circumstances are leading them. These people don't yet know they have both the ability and the authority to release the power in their mouths by declaring God's Word and His will, just as Jesus did.

In the book of Luke we see the account of how Jesus spoke to a fever: *Jesus left the synagogue and went to the home of Simon. Now Simon's mother-in-law was suffering from a high fever, and they asked Jesus to help her. So he bent over her and rebuked the fever, and it left her. She got up at once and began to wait on them* (Luke 4:38–39). Jesus told the fever to go, and it left. We know it was God's will that the woman be healed because Jesus was speaking God's will over her.

God's will for healing hasn't changed; it's His will that we too experience the healing Jesus has already provided for us. The prophet Isaiah spoke the following present-tense words about the coming Messiah: *And by his stripes we are healed* (Isaiah 53:5 NKJV). Peter spoke in the past tense when he said the same about the risen Jesus: *by whose stripes you were healed* (1 Peter 2:24 NKJV). In other words, the Old and New Testaments both confirm that healing is and has always been the will of God for His people.

In the book of Luke, we find this account of Jesus speaking forth God's will in the face of religious tradition:

> On a Sabbath Jesus was teaching in one of the synagogues, and a woman was there who had been crippled by a spirit for eighteen years. She was bent over and could not straighten up at all. When Jesus saw

> her, he called her forward and said to her, "Woman, you are set free from your infirmity." Then he put his hands on her, and immediately she straightened up and praised God.
>
> Indignant because Jesus had healed on the Sabbath, the synagogue leader said to the people, "There are six days for work. So come and be healed on those days, not the Sabbath."
>
> The Lord answered him, "You hypocrites! Doesn't each of you on the Sabbath untie your ox or donkey from the stall and lead it out to give it water? Then should not this woman, a daughter of Abraham, whom Satan has kept bound for eighteen long years, be set free on the Sabbath day from what bound her?"
>
> When he said this, all his opponents were humiliated, but the people were delighted with all the wonderful things he was doing (Luke 13:10–17).

Notice the woman had been crippled *by a spirit* for eighteen years. The King James Version identifies this spirit as a "spirit of infirmity." It's important to understand the demonic realm is not the cause of every sickness. Sickness is part of a fallen world, and God has given us the tools to resist sickness. However, in this case a spirit of infirmity *had* caused the woman's condition. When Jesus said, "Woman, you are set free from your infirmity," He was declaring and establishing the will of God. We too can declare and establish the will of God, for the Word of

God makes this promise: *You will also declare a thing, and it will be established for you; so light will shine on your ways* (Job 22:28 NKJV).

We see Jesus again speaking the Word of God in power, this time to set free a demon-possessed man in the region of Gerasenes:

> When Jesus got out of the boat, a man with an impure spirit came from the tombs to meet him. This man lived in the tombs, and no one could bind him anymore, not even with a chain.
>
> When he saw Jesus from a distance, he ran and fell on his knees in front of him. He shouted at the top of his voice, "What do you want with me, Jesus, Son of the Most High God? In God's name don't torture me!" For Jesus had said to him, "Come out of this man, you impure spirit!"
>
> Then Jesus asked him, "What is your name?"
>
> "My name is Legion," he replied, "for we are many." And he begged Jesus again and again not to send them out of the area (Mark 5:2, 6–10).

Jesus never wavered after He commanded the spirit to come out of the man, though the Spirit attempted to resist Him. The principal demonic spirit, Legion, recognized Jesus as the Son of the Most High God and begged Jesus not to send him and the others out of the area. Legion asked instead to be allowed to go into a herd of pigs. When Jesus gave the spirits permission to enter the pigs, the entire herd of about two thousand rushed down the steep bank into the lake and drowned.

Jesus commissioned His followers to go into all the world and preach the gospel, saying, *"And these signs will accompany those who believe: In my name they will drive out demons"* (Mark 16:17). Jesus didn't say the signs would accompany only preachers; He said they would accompany those who *believe*—that's you and me! As Jesus is, so are we in this world.

PRAYING GOD'S PROMISES

As believers, we may view the act of praying God's promises as a New Testament practice; however, we see this principle in effect in the Old Testament as well. The Word of God says, *Elijah was a human being, even as we are. He prayed earnestly that it would not rain, and it did not rain on the land for three and a half years. Again he prayed, and the heavens gave rain, and the earth produced its crops* (James 5:17–18).

Elijah was an Old Testament prophet who lived at a time when the Spirit of God rested on a few select people—unlike our time when God's Spirit is available to all who accept Jesus as Lord and Savior. God appointed Elijah to speak to the nation of Israel at a time when God's people were not wholeheartedly following Him. In other words, they liked some things about God, but they also liked some things about the world. So they had decided to follow both.

The Lord sent Elijah to Ahab, king of Israel, of whom the Bible says, *Ahab son of Omri did more evil in the eyes of the Lord than any of those before him* (1 Kings 16:30). Elijah said, *"As the Lord, the God of Israel, lives, whom I serve, there will be neither dew nor rain in the next few years except at my word"* (1 Kings 17:1).

The Lord miraculously provided food and water for Elijah throughout the drought, until it was time for Elijah to again speak forth God's will to Ahab:

> After a long time, in the third year, the word of the Lord came to Elijah: "Go and present yourself to Ahab, and I will send rain on the land." So Elijah went to present himself to Ahab.
>
> And Elijah said to Ahab, "Go, eat and drink, for there is the sound of a heavy rain." So Ahab went off to eat and drink, but Elijah climbed to the top of Carmel, bent down to the ground and put his face between his knees.
>
> "Go and look toward the sea," he told his servant. And he went up and looked.
>
> "There is nothing there," he said.
>
> Seven times Elijah said, "Go back."
>
> The seventh time the servant reported, "A cloud as small as a man's hand is rising from the sea."
>
> So Elijah said, "Go and tell Ahab, 'Hitch up your chariot and go down before the rain stops you.'"

> Meanwhile, the sky grew black with clouds, the wind rose, a heavy rain started falling and Ahab rode off to Jezreel. The power of the Lord came on Elijah and, tucking his cloak into his belt, he ran ahead of Ahab all the way to Jezreel (1 Kings 18:1, 41–46).

As Elijah spoke forth God's words, the power of prayer in Elijah's mouth resulted in an absence of rain for three years. Then, when Elijah prayed again, the heavens gave rain that brought forth the earth's crops. I particularly like the words used in the book of James to describe Elijah as "a human being, even as we are" (see James 5:17). It shows us that as human beings made in God's image, when we speak the Word of God to our circumstances, they *have* to change.

Speaking God's Word aloud is the most powerful thing we can do with our mouths.

I find it interesting that the Scripture says Elijah prayed *earnestly* (see James 5:17). We may read Elijah's story and equate earnest prayer with his zealous action of bending down and putting his face between his knees seven times. But God doesn't see it that way; He equates earnest prayer with speaking His will and His Word.

Remember, God had already determined there would first be a drought, and then after three years it would rain. He's God; He can do anything He wants. So what was the point in Elijah's praying? Elijah was releasing the will and Word of God into the earth through his mouth. He was releasing God's creative power into the situation. As I said before, nothing in this life happens without prayer. Prayer that represents God's Word.

Interestingly, it didn't rain the first time Elijah prayed—or the second, third, fourth, fifth, or sixth time he bowed down to the ground and put his face between his knees. Elijah had a promise from God. He knew what was about to rain, yet he prayed earnestly—speaking forth the Word of God—seven times before the promise came to pass.

Speaking God's Word aloud is the most powerful thing we can do with our mouths, and the enemy knows it. This is why he often keeps us busy doing good things, to the point we don't have time to spend in the Word of God, where we find the promises we are to declare.

When I was first learning about speaking forth the promises of God into my own life, one of the Bible verses I used as a foundation for my prayers was John 14:12–14. In that passage Jesus said, *"Very truly I tell you, whoever believes in me will do the works I have been doing, and they will do even greater things than these, because I am going to the Father. And I will do whatever you ask in my name, so that the Father may be glorified in the Son. You may ask me for anything in my name, and I will do it."*

I remember reading those verses, doing just as Jesus had said, and then getting frustrated when what I'd asked of God didn't happen. I know I'm not the only person to have experienced this frustration in my prayer life. To understand why prayers may go unanswered, let's look at the word *ask*. Jesus said He would do whatever we ask in His name; therefore, could it be we are not looking at the word *ask* correctly?

We generally associate the word *ask* with a question: May I have another piece of pizza? Can you help me? What time is it? But this is not the meaning of the word used by Jesus in the original language. The meaning of the word Jesus used was "request; petition; call for; require."

When Jesus said we are to ask, then we are to request, petition, call for, and require without any sense of uneasiness or self-doubt. When we call for something from God, we are not commanding Him; rather, we are approaching Him with confidence, fully persuaded He will release to us that which we have asked of Him.

As a mother, it's my pleasure to release to each of my three daughters those things they ask of me. My girls and I are approximately the same height and clothing size; therefore, it's not uncommon for them to go "shopping" in my closet for something to wear on a particular occasion.

A typical shopping excursion looks something like this: As one of my daughters is walking out of the closet with a dress in hand she asks, "Hey, Mom, may I wear this black dress of yours?" I always say, "Sure." Why wouldn't my girls first come to me and ask permission to wear my clothing? Why would they pull a dress from my closet without first hearing my answer? They know I desire to release my clothing to them; they know I'm generous and I want to bless them. When they ask something of me, they are fully persuaded and confident I will grant their requests.

Jesus said, *"If you abide in Me, and My words abide in you, you will ask what you desire, and it shall be done for you"* (John 15:7). That word *abide* means "to live." Jesus didn't say, "If you visit Me once in a while, you can ask for what you want." He said that we are to be in His life and He in ours. When He told us His words are to abide in us, He was speaking of His ways, His character, and who He really is, actually living in us.

I can imagine Jesus saying, "To have My words abiding in you means you've taken the time to figure out who I am. You've spent some time in My Word and seen how much I love you, how much I have for you. My words are living in you; they are who you are. Therefore, ask what you desire, and it will be done for you."

When we abide in God's Word and His presence, we cultivate an environment that makes daily conversation with God easy, as He speaks to us from His Word. When we abide in Jesus and His words abide in us, our hearts literally become one with the Father's. His desires become our desires; they are meshed. All of a sudden, we desire the things He desires; therefore, when we ask what we desire, we're asking what He desires because we are one with Him. We see this principle beautifully expressed in the marriage relationship. Jesus said, *"The two will become one flesh. So they are no longer two, but one flesh"* (Mark 10:8).

God hungers for this kind of relationship with us. His desire is that we become so like Him that we actually see our lives through His perspective, free from all shame and limitations, and exercising the power of prayer through our mouths.

KEYS TO POWERFUL PRAYER

Most of us remember learning the classic eighteenth-century childhood prayer "Now I Lay Me Down to Sleep." As we grew older, we may have memorized what has come to be known as "The Lord's Prayer," which Jesus taught His disciples. Sadly, many believers have not developed their prayer lives beyond these two prayers and, perhaps, the giving of thanks at mealtime.

We've come to understand God's will for us is that we exercise dominion in this life and that we do so through the words we speak. We know the source of powerful prayer is praying forth God's Word, yet we may wonder, *How can I be certain that my prayers will be answered?* I believe the responsibility for getting our prayers answered rests firmly with us and that we can access that answered prayer by utilizing three important keys. Those keys are *confidence, humility, and consistency.*

Confidence is a word we understand to mean "full trust; belief in the powers, trustworthiness, or reliability of another." The Word of God says, *This is the confidence we have in approaching God: that if we ask anything according to his will, he hears us* (1 John 5:14). In this instance the word *confidence* means "assurance."

God wants us to be assured of the fact that He loves us, and confident in the power and authority He's given us. The way we become confident in Him is by spending time in His Word. This is where we learn to trust in His reliability and the veracity of His Word.

When I meditate on the verse in 1 John that talks about our confidence in God, I recall an incident from my childhood. My brothers were in elementary school at the time, and they were having frequent trouble with another boy who bullied them as

> Our humility creates an environment where prayer becomes powerful in our mouths.

they walked home from school. My dad was fit to be tied when they told him, but then he came up with a plan. "Tomorrow I'm going to follow you as you walk home from school, but I'm going to stay out of sight. I'm going to take care of this bully," he said.

The next day my brothers weren't fearful or timid as they began their walk home; rather, they were confident in our father's love and fully assured he was going to take care of them. Sure enough, the bully showed up and started taunting my brothers. But instead of running toward home in fear, they stood their ground. That's when my dad jumped out from behind the bushes and scared the bully so badly that he literally had to go home and change his pants.

So what was the difference in my brothers' demeanor from one day to the next? The first day they were fearful; the second day they were fully confident. They knew our father loved them, and they trusted in his full power and authority to handle the situation. Likewise, we can be fully confident in our heavenly Father's love for us as we move forward in life in His power and authority.

The second key to receiving answered prayer, *humility*, is the quality of being *humble*, which means "modest; not proud or arrogant." I believe one of the reasons we do not see our prayers answered is that we lack humility. Instead of submitting to God's will and His Word, we ask Him to bless *our* plans and *our* ways. God won't bless us in such instances because He knows that blessing something we're doing our way may lead to our destruction.

God said, "*If my people, who are called by my name, will humble themselves and pray and seek my face and turn from their wicked ways, then I will hear from heaven, and I will forgive their sin and will heal their land* (2 Chronicles 7:14). In this verse the word *humble* means "to bend the knee; to come into subjection." Isn't this just what Elijah did when he prayed on Carmel?

We are God's people, and He is saying to us today that if we will humble ourselves, if we will turn from doing things our way instead of His way, and if we will seek His face and pray, then He will forgive our sin and heal our land. Our physical bodies are land; God will heal our bodies. He will heal our cities, and He will heal our country. Our humility creates an environment where prayer becomes powerful in our mouths.

The third key for receiving answered prayer is *consistency.* We understand *consistency* to mean "steadfast adherence to the same principles or course; agreement, harmony, or compatibility." If we think about driving a vehicle, we know as long as we keep a foot on the pedal, we will keep moving in the desired direction. When we remove that consistent pressure from the pedal, the vehicle will begin to slow down and eventually stop. It's the same with prayer: as we are consistent to spend time in the Word and in conversations with God, we keep moving, growing, and experiencing tremendous breakthroughs.

Consistency with God causes us to see things from His perspective, which then causes us to pray even more powerful prayers. Consistency also solidifies God's truth in our hearts.

There are times when we hear a truth about God and believe it, and then assume that truth is working in our lives. But this isn't always so. A number of years ago I attended a meeting in which the speaker was talking about healing, something I'd not yet heard about. At that time I was struggling with an incurable illness, so the message on healing was music to my ears. In my head I believed what the speaker said; however, because for years I'd heard that God doesn't heal, that wrong information had solidified in my heart. Only after spending consistent time meditating on healing scriptures did the truth about healing make it to my heart—and I was healed!

Powerful prayer doesn't just happen. It requires confidence, humility, and consistency—but its benefits are significant. When we humble ourselves and say, "We want more of You, God; we want more of You in our lives, in our churches, and in our cities," we put ourselves in position to move to a new level in Him. A level in which we will see His manifested power in both our own lives and the lives of those around us.

DISCUSSION QUESTIONS

If God has given us dominion on earth, why then do we have to battle for that dominion? (See Ephesians 6:12.)

How did Jesus demonstrate the release of power in behalf of Simon's mother-in-law? (See Luke 4:38–39.)

How can we know with certainty God will hear and answer our prayers that are in line with His will? (See John 15:7; 1 John 5:14.)

How do we release God's will in the earth?

CHAPTER FOUR

THE PRESENCE OF GOD IS IN YOUR MOUTH

But thou art holy, O thou that inhabitest the praises of Israel.

PSALMS 22:3 (KJV)

I'm so grateful for the privilege of working with my husband, James. We work together in the church and also in business. I enjoy working alongside him because we are alike in many ways.

James and I are both producers, in that we each want to make a positive difference in our world. Oftentimes when I'm in our church office, I'll ask our staff, "So did we change the world today?" Invariably they'll say, "Yes, we changed the world today." Knowing we've made a positive contribution to the lives of others gives James and me great pleasure.

I particularly enjoy our evenings at home together as we're closing down the activities of the day. We're usually in the same room while we wrap up projects on our phones or iPads, our minds engrossed in the satisfaction that comes from a day spent working with God. But if I stop for a moment and say, "Baby, I just love you. You're so amazing, and I appreciate you so much," something happens. The atmosphere changes, and we become aware of each other in an intimate way, as husband and wife rather than coworkers. This change of mind-set is brought about with just a few words spoken out loud.

Let's look at this different mindfulness in the context of our relationship with God. When it comes to the Lord, He's omnipresent, which means He is present everywhere at the same time. But when we take the time to adore Him and give Him words of gratitude, when we worship Him and give Him thanks, desiring only to see His face, something changes. Our simple words of affirmation and adoration usher in His manifested presence.

Scripture cites many examples of people who called on God, who worshiped and adored Him in various situations, bringing about His manifested presence. Their adoration and worship resulted in military victories, breakthroughs, wisdom, and supernatural peace.

We've already learned that within our mouths we hold our futures, our hearts, and great power. We are now going to learn about the amazing connection between our mouths and the manifested presence of God—and what that presence brings. To understand this connection, let's take a look at a familiar Bible story about two of Jesus' disciples: Paul, a church planter, and Silas, another member of the early church. We pick up the narrative immediately after the two men had been arrested together for preaching the gospel.

> The crowd joined in the attack against Paul and Silas, and the magistrates ordered them to be stripped and beaten with rods. After they had been severely flogged, they were thrown into prison, and the jailer was commanded to guard them carefully. When he received these orders, he put them in the inner cell and fastened their feet in stocks.
>
> About midnight Paul and Silas were praying and singing hymns to God, and the other prisoners were listening to them. Suddenly there was such a violent earthquake that the foundations of the prison were shaken. At once the prison doors flew open, and everyone's chains came loose. The jailer woke up, and when he saw the prison doors open, he drew his sword and was about to kill himself because he thought the prisoners had escaped. But Paul shouted, "Don't harm yourself! We are all here!"
>
> The jailer called for lights, rushed in and fell trembling before Paul and Silas. Then he brought them out and asked, "Sirs, what must I do to be saved?" (Acts 16:22–30).

Not only had Paul and Silas been severely beaten, they were also put in stocks and thrown into the inner dungeon. During that day, when people were placed in stocks, it was done in such a way as to cause pain. In addition to being in a physically painful situation, the prisoners were sitting in mire. I can only imagine the stench in that cell, and then I think about the scampering sounds made by the rats as they ran through the place. Paul and Silas were in a bad situation.

The two men were being persecuted for their faith, yet Paul and Silas were praying and singing as the other prisoners listened to them around midnight. Notice they weren't complain-

They were invoking the presence of God as they magnified His great name.

ing, groaning, or verbalizing anger at God; they were praying and singing hymns. They were invoking the presence of God as they magnified His great name. They understood something about the Lord, for they had probably read this verse from the book of Psalms many times: *But thou art holy, O thou that inhabitest the praises of Israel* (Psalms 22:3 KJV). Paul and Silas understood God's presence comes into a place of worship.

The Bible says that the earthquake hit suddenly, and in an instant the prison doors flew open and its foundations were shaken. The jailer assumed the prisoners had escaped; therefore, he prepared to kill himself. According to Roman law, if a soldier lost a prisoner, he had to take his own life, or else it would be taken from him. But when Paul shouted for the jailer not to harm himself, in essence he was saying, "You matter; your life is valuable." The jailer recognized the supernatural presence of God that had manifested as a result of prayer and praise, and immediately asked what he must do to be saved.

When people read an account like this in the Scripture, they may think, *Oh that supernatural stuff was just for them. It doesn't happen like that today.* But they are wrong; the supernatural manifestation of God's presence is indeed for us today. God Himself said, *"I the Lord do not change"* (Malachi 3:6). The Bible says, *Remember your leaders, who spoke the word of God to you. Consider the outcome of their way of life and imitate their faith. Jesus Christ is the same yesterday and today and forever* (Hebrews 13:7–8). We have the same access to the presence of God that Paul and Silas had.

When we establish the presence of God through the prayers and praises we offer with our mouths, we tap into all the benefits His presence brings: deliverance, vindication, protection, direction, joy, peace, and the awareness of our need for God. Let's look at each of these benefits individually.

GOD'S PRESENCE BRINGS DELIVERANCE

In part 3 we examined how Jesus taught His disciples to pray, declaring, *"Your kingdom come. Your will be done on earth as it is in heaven"* (Luke 11:2 NKJV). Jesus concluded His prayer with these words: *"But deliver us from the evil one"* (verse 4).

We see a picture of this deliverance for Paul and Silas when the prison doors opened and their chains were broken: the presence of God set them free. The psalmist David said, *I will give thanks to you, Lord, with all my heart; I will tell of all your wonderful deeds. I will be glad and rejoice in you; I will sing the praises of your name, O Most High. My enemies turn back; they stumble and perish before you* (Psalms 9:1–3). Do these words sound like praise and worship? Do they sound like adoration of God? Yes—and as a result of David's speaking forth God's praise with his mouth, David's enemies turned back; they stumbled and perished! God's presence brought deliverance.

There have been multiple times when I've physically struggled with physical distress in my body, but then as I worshiped, the pain or symptoms would leave. On one occasion I had such severe pain in my lower abdomen that I could hardly move. I needed to move because it was the day of my daughter's wedding! As I was sitting down, simply worshiping God and meditating on His goodness, all the pain left.

GOD'S PRESENCE BRINGS VINDICATION

We may not always understand all that takes place in the unseen realm, yet the Bible tells us, by faith, we have access to what happens there: *Now faith is the substance of things hoped for, the evidence of things not seen* (Hebrews 11:1 NKJV). When we are worshiping God and His presence manifests, vindication occurs in the demonic realm.

Just as God has plans and purposes for our lives, so the enemy has his own plans and purposes for us. He may have had destructive plans set in place against our lives for years, but in that moment of our praising God and ushering in His presence, the enemy's plans are destroyed. Demons stagger and draw back, and we are vindicated.

I once heard the vindication process described like this: When we are in a trial and things are not going as we expected, despite the fact that we have exercised our faith, we need to worship God. The sound of our worship and praise, which comes from sheer faith in His power, provision, and faithfulness, is to the enemy the sound of a funeral dirge. He hears the death knell for his plans against us and thinks, *I can't believe those Christians; here they go again!*

This illustration is an accurate depiction of Paul and Silas's situation. The enemy thought, *I've got them now,* but God wasn't finished. In their praise, worship, and adoration of God, Paul and Silas saw His presence manifested. The enemy *had* to draw back; he had to run in terror.

Satan does not like to be around the manifested presence of God, and he certainly doesn't like to be around worship, because he knows what they bring: vindication. The word *vindication* means "justice; a plan; defense; to clear as from accusation." The Word of God says, *Let my vindication come from Your presence; let Your eyes look on the things that are upright* (Psalms 17:2).

The presence of God brings vindication.

GOD'S PRESENCE BRINGS PROTECTION

God has created us to live the wonderful lives He has prepared for us, yet the enemy is always working against God's plans. The enemy does this primarily by speaking lies contrary to the truth of who God created us to be and how He intends us to live.

These lies from the enemy are so subtle and crafty that we often are not aware of what is happening to us. However, one minute in the presence of God can cause the enemy's lies to fall away, because God's presence brings protection.

God has made a way to protect us from the attacks of the enemy. The Word of God says, *You are my hiding place; you will protect me from trouble and surround me with songs of deliverance* (Psalms 32:7). Sometimes we have to sing to get our deliverance. I experienced this truth firsthand in 2002 when my first husband passed away.

Prior to that tragic event, I'd established the habit of entering the presence of God and seeking His face on a daily basis. After reading how Jesus rose early in the morning to seek the Father, I reasoned, *Well, if Jesus had to seek the Father, then I really have to seek the Father.*

It's amazing how anything going on in the realm of the soul—the mind, will, and emotions—impacts our physical health. As the mother of three young daughters and the wife of a man who was seriously ill, both my soul and body had become depleted and weak. But I always knew where to get the help I needed to see me through each day: I spent time in my study, reading the

Word of God and worshiping Him.

But one particular morning when I entered my study, I felt an evil, demonic presence come into the room. I immediately recognized it as a spirit of grief, which my friend Bishop Keith Butler had warned might come against me. This spirit had nothing to do with the mourning we experience at a time of loss; rather, the spirit brought a sense of hopelessness that made me feel I didn't want to live anymore.

With our mouths we invoke the very presence of God, and with that presence comes His protection.

God's Word describes this kind of grief, saying, *Worldly grief (the hopeless sorrow that is characteristic of the pagan world) is deadly [breeding and ending in death]* (2 Corinthians 7:10 AMP). I knew the spirit I was facing was demonic because I literally felt something was squeezing my neck, taking the life out of me. The enemy knows when we are vulnerable, and I was vulnerable. I immediately went back to my training and knowledge that in God's presence is protection.

I began to worship the Lord, singing lyrics from Psalms 32, even as I continued to sense the enemy taking my breath from me. "*You are my hiding place. You always fill my heart with songs of deliverance. Whenever I am afraid, I will trust in you; I will trust in you. Let the weak say 'I am strong' in the strength of the Lord."* Within twenty minutes that evil presence had lifted.

With our mouths we invoke the very presence of God, and with that presence comes His protection.

GOD'S PRESENCE BRINGS DIRECTION

We all need God's direction in our lives. As the pastor of a growing church, I need God's direction. Likewise, my husband and I need His direction for our businesses and our family. What a blessing it is to know God's presence brings the direction we need in every area of our lives.

In Acts 13:1–3, we see how the early church in the city of Antioch experienced this truth: *Now in the church at Antioch there were prophets and teachers: Barnabas, Simeon called Niger, Lucius of Cyrene, Manaen (who had been brought up with Herod the tetrarch) and Saul. While they were worshiping the Lord and fasting, the Holy Spirit said, "Set apart for me Barnabas and Saul for the work to which I have called them." So after they had fasted and prayed, they placed their hands on them and sent them off*.

What were those men doing? They were all gathered in a room with no agenda other than to seek God's face; they were there to worship Him. And in the midst of their worshiping God, the presence of the Holy Spirit manifested with specific direction that launched Barnabas and Saul (who became known as Paul) into a world-changing ministry.

Can it be that, in surrendering to our individual places of

worship, we believers actually solidify God's purposes in our lives? Based on my experience, the answer is yes. I cannot list all of the wonderful things going on in our church that have come about as a result of our simply ministering to the Lord in the morning. Out of that place of worship, God reveals what He wants us to do and where He wants us to go.

If you are in need of direction from God, I can assure you, all you need to do is spend some time worshiping Him. I've learned it's impossible to both worship the Lord and worry at about direction or answers for my life at the same time. Worship will trump worry every time!

GOD'S PRESENCE BRINGS JOY

The Bible is clear about the connection between God's presence and the impartation of joy: *You will show me the path of life; in your presence is fullness of joy* (Psalms 16:11 NKJV). The word *fullness* means "satisfaction; abundance; overflowing."

Notice this verse does not say there is fullness of *happiness* in God's presence. Happiness is not a bad thing; however, happiness is determined by our circumstances. Joy has nothing to do with what's happening in the natural realm; rather, joy is a supernatural impartation inside us that enables us to walk through the most difficult of situations.

The Scripture says, "*Do not grieve, for the joy of the Lord is your strength*" (Nehemiah 8:10). When do we need strength? When we're going through the situations and circumstances of life. In the presence of God, His joy sustains us. There is an actual transfer of joy from God's Spirit to us that literally strengthens us. Nothing has changed on the outside, but we've changed on the inside. We are looking at our circumstances through the eye of faith.

I've awakened countless times, my mind being bombarded with insurmountable situations I am facing. I can actually feel a weight that saps my strength. However, as I go into His presence and stay there for a while, something changes in me. Joy comes, and I am strengthened.

Let's look at Psalms 16:11 in its entirety: *You will show me the path of life; in Your presence is fullness of joy; at Your right hand are pleasures evermore* (NKJV). God wants us to enjoy our lives, to take pleasure in them.

God's presence brings us peace in any circumstance or situation.

I was raised in a church that believed the poorer you were, the more holy you were. I don't know where they got that idea, because it's not in the Bible. The belief may *sound* reasonable, but it's not true. Much of human reasoning sounds good but doesn't line up with anything God has said. Human reasoning can destroy lives.

Here's the bottom line: if you think you can find enjoyment

doing things the world's way, you are being played by the devil. The only way to find fullness of joy is in the presence of God.

GOD'S PRESENCE BRINGS PEACE

All we have to do is open a newspaper or turn on the television to see the one critical thing lacking in our world today is peace. The world has accepted chaos and turmoil as the norm; medical science has even determined that 99 percent of all sickness and disease is stress related.

Many of us are dying on the inside as a result of mind-related matters that breed stress and anxiety, even though God has already given us the remedy for dealing with such matters. His Word says, *Be anxious for nothing, but in everything let your requests be made known to God; and the peace of God, which surpasses all understanding, will guard your hearts and minds through Jesus Christ* (Philippians 4:6–7). This verse doesn't say we are to be anxious for some things; it says we are to be anxious for *nothing*. Why is it important we not worry *at all*? Because worry can shorten our lives. When we are worried about something, we are in a continual state of anxiety that affects the soul: the mind, will, and emotions. And what happens in the soul eventually affects the body.

When we *choose* to refuse anxiety and stress, and *choose* instead to enter the presence of God through prayer, the Scripture says His peace will guard our hearts and minds. God's presence brings us peace in any circumstance or situation. And that peace gives us great confidence, for the Bible says, *This is the confidence we have in approaching God: that if we ask anything according to his will, he hears us* (1 John 5:14).

Jesus comforted His disciples prior to His crucifixion, saying, *"Peace I leave with you; my peace I give to you. I do not give to you as the world gives. Do not let your hearts be troubled and do not be afraid"* (John 14:27). In other words, Jesus was telling the twelve, "Everybody is looking for peace, but there's no way you can find it in the world. This is why I'm giving you true peace—My peace."

When you're in a storm of life, you can enter God's presence with a heart and mouth of thanksgiving. The peace that comes with God's presence will surround your heart and mind, giving you the confidence to know everything is going to be okay—because He is with you.

GOD'S PRESENCE BRINGS THE AWARENESS OF OUR NEED FOR HIM

At the beginning of this chapter, we read the story of Paul and Silas's being locked in a prison. We saw that when the presence of God freed them from their chains and opened the prison doors, the jailer fell before the two men and said, "Sirs, what must I do to be saved?"

God's presence in that prison made the jailer aware of his need for God.

I was raised in a religious system that never taught me about a God who died for me and that I could get to my heavenly Father by simply accepting His Son, Jesus. I thought I couldn't get to God because I'd learned I had to behave a certain way and do things a certain way to be part of His family. That belief was what religion taught me.

But one day my family was invited to attend a church very different from ours. When we arrived, the place was crowded with people waving their hands as the band onstage played its music. I'd been taught that any church with a band and a stage was of the devil and was a cult.

As I looked around the auditorium, I saw people praising God, dancing, and having a good time; they were rocking it out. At first I thought, *This is ridiculous; I need to get out of here.* But then something hit me, and all I wanted to do was cry. I didn't realize it at the time, but the "something" that hit me was the presence of God. When His presence manifested, that religious spirit left, and all I could say was, "I need God. I need God!" As a fish needs water, so I needed God. That's when I gave my heart to Him.

When the presence of God manifests, those who do not yet know Him suddenly become aware of their need for Him.

God's presence is so powerful and so amazing. Our gracious God invites you and me to enjoy and engage His presence. He wants to be a part of everything we do. You may be in need of direction or deliverance regarding a situation right now. Maybe you're up all hours of the night experiencing anxiety, and you're desperate for joy and peace. It's all available in God's presence.

Right now, I believe God is saying, "Come into My presence, draw near to Me. There you will find answers to your questions and rest for your soul."

SEEK GOD'S PRESENCE DAILY

My husband and I understand the vital importance of seeking God's presence on a daily basis; therefore, we agreed early in our marriage that we would begin each day with worship. There is great power that comes from a husband and wife's coming into agreement in prayer and worship. The Bible talks about this power of agreement, saying, *Do two walk together unless they have agreed to do so?* (Amos 3:3). Jesus said, *"Again, truly I tell you that if two of you on earth agree about anything they ask for, it will be done for them by my Father in heaven"* (Matthew 18:19).

When James and I rise each morning, the first thing we do is put on worship music. Our minds may want to go to issues from the previous day, decisions that need to be made, and legitimate issues that need our attention at the church or in our business. But once we enter that place of worship, our minds settle down as we begin to sing and worship the Lord.

In that place of worship, the presence of God manifests, bringing the clarity, strength, wisdom, peace, and joy we need to walk victoriously through the upcoming day.

Perhaps you are in place now where you need answers and direction from God, but they seem slow in coming. You think you are waiting on God, but could it be that God is actually waiting on you? Could it be that He is waiting for you to surrender to Him, to open your mouth with praise in a way that will usher in His presence? I hear Jesus saying, "Go into your prayer closet and just hang with me."

Approach your worship time with this attitude: I *get* to go into the presence of God. I *get* to hear from heaven. I *get* to receive God's direction and answers, and I *get* to go on a divine journey today. With this kind of faith and expectancy, you can rest assured that you'll never be disappointed.

It's been twenty-seven years since I experienced my healing after God showed me how to subdue my earth—my body—with the words of my mouth. I've learned so much since then about God and His Word as my life journey has taken me to mountaintops and through valleys. I've experienced both devastating defeats and miraculous victories, but through it all God has been faithful to me and to His Word.

Most importantly, I've learned that the authority of the words of my mouth stems from my relationship with Jesus: the more I know Him, the more powerful my words are. The authority we have in Jesus is directly related to the depth of our relationship with Him. Because He submitted to His Father and spoke only His Father's words rather than depending on Himself, Jesus' words were filled with power and authority. He said, *"For I have not spoken on My own authority; but the Father who sent Me gave Me a command, what I should say and what I should speak … Therefore, whatever I speak, just as the Father has told Me, so I speak"* (John 12:49–50).

The depth of our relationship with Jesus determines the level of authority our words carry here on earth. When Jesus said, *I will give you the keys of the kingdom of heaven; whatever you bind on earth will be bound in heaven, and whatever you loose on earth will be loosed in heaven"* (Matthew 16:19), He was not talking about a physical set of keys. In essence, Jesus was saying, "The keys to living a victorious life on earth are in your mouth. The keys to establishing dominion in this life are in your mouth. The keys to healing and wholeness are in your mouth. The keys to moving spiritual substance into the natural realm are in your mouth, and the keys to destroying the works of the enemy are in your mouth."

Time and time again throughout His earthly ministry, Jesus used His mouth to establish God's will in every situation and circumstance He encountered. From healing the sick, to calming storms, to raising the dead, to casting out demons, Jesus used nothing more than His words to usher in the signs and wonders that followed His ministry. And yet He said, *Very truly I tell you, whoever believes in me will do the works I have been doing, and they will do even greater things than these, because I am going to the Father* (John 14:12).

You and I are the believers Jesus spoke about. We are the ones who hold the keys of the kingdom in our generation. We are the ones who can use our mouths to frame our individual destinies and bring forth God's manifested power and presence in the earth. But the choice is ours: we can choose to believe God's Word and speak it into our lives and circumstances, or we can allow our words to lead us the way of the world.

I've written this book to give you the biblical truth and practical wisdom you need to experience the wonderful life God has planned for you to the fullest. But it all boils down to this one question: *what's in your mouth?*

DISCUSSION QUESTIONS

What assurance do we have that the supernatural manifestation of God's presence is available for us today? (See Malachi 3:6; Hebrews 13:7–8.)

How did Paul and Silas cause the presence of God to manifest in their prison cell? (See Psalms 22:3.)

When we are in the midst of a battle, how can we bring God's presence into our situation? (See Psalms 9:1–3.)

In what ways does the "power of agreement" impact the lives of those who choose to exercise it? (See Amos 3:3; Matthew 18:19.)

DOMINION CONFESSIONS

FOR PHYSICAL HEALING

Father, I boldly come before You—not on the basis of my own merits but through what Jesus accomplished on the cross and through the resurrection. I am so grateful that You considered dying for me a worthy cause. I'm so grateful that You've come to live inside me through the Holy Spirit. My body is the temple of the Holy Spirit. I'm so grateful that You love me. (See John 16:23, 14:16–17; 1 Corinthians 3:16.)

Father, I thank You that in Your great mercy You have *forgiven* me of any sin I may have committed. As You have forgiven and shown me mercy, I choose to forgive all who have done wrong to me. I thank You I am free from the power of unforgiveness, strife, bitterness, and envy. I'm dead to sin. I give no place to the enemy in my life. I see myself cleansed and in right standing with You. I see You loving me. (See 1 John 1:9; Colossians 1:21–22; Ephesians 4:27.)

Father, I thank You that You have given me *dominion* over my physical body, which is made from the dust of the earth. You said to subdue the earth. Out of Your great love, You have given me authority to use Your name to cause everything in my body to be as You created it to be: full of life and health. Body, you are healthy and strong, the way God made you to be. I see myself strong and healthy. (See Genesis 1:26–28, 2:7; John 14:13.)

I speak Your Word, which is medicine to all my flesh, and subdue my body to health, for You have said that life and death are in the power of my tongue. I speak words of life, and they produce life in my physical body. The medicine of 1 Peter 2:24, by Your wounds I am healed, is flowing through my body. I *see* this medicine flowing in every cell, organ, and tissue of my body. (See Proverbs 4:22, 18:21.)

Jesus, You took my sickness and pain; You bore them on the cross. What You bore in Your body, I need not bear. I refuse to allow sickness to live in my body. Body, I *see* you well in Jesus' name. (See Isaiah 53:4.)

Father, You said You sent Your Word and You healed me. Jesus, You are the Word; You live in me. Your life in me is supernatural, promoting healing to all my flesh. The same Spirit that raised Christ from the dead dwells in me and quickens, gives life to, all my mortal body. Body, I *see* you responding to the very life of God that lives in me. (See Psalms 118:17; John 1:24; Romans 8:11.)

I bless You, Lord, with all my soul. I forget not Your benefits toward me. You have forgiven all my iniquities and healed all my diseases. You have redeemed my life from destruction and crowned me with lovingkindness and tender mercies. You satisfy my mouth with good things, and my youth is renewed. I *see* my body young and vibrant with health. (See Psalms 103:2–5.)

No weapon formed against me can prosper, for God is for me, not against me. A thousand fall at my side, ten thousand at my right hand, but sickness and disease cannot come near me, for the Lord is my refuge. I see myself kept, surrounded, and shielded by the Word of God. I *see* myself shielded in God's presence. (See Isaiah 54:17; Romans 8:30; Psalms 91:7–10; 1 Peter 1:5.)

I speak to you, *immune system*. Because God's supernatural Spirit lives in me, you are strong. You are not compromised in any way. You are operating in perfection, as God created you to be. Immune system, you are warding off all forms of sickness and disease. I *see* my whole immune system supporting my body with complete health.

Bone marrow, I speak to you in Jesus' name. You are producing healthy, pure blood that carries healing to all my physical body. I command my veins and arteries to be open and to carry to every part of my body Jesus' life-giving, healthy blood that is full of His Spirit.

Cells, I say to you in Jesus' name, you are filled with the supernatural life of God. You can't help but be whole and strong, for God is in you. I *see* my cells pumping with the very life of God.

Holy Spirit, You are the orchestrator of life. You are quickening my organs, my tissues, my joints, and my bones with Your supernatural life. I refuse any malfunction in my body. Body, you are whole, completely whole. I *see* you, body, in perfect health. (See Romans 8:11.)

Jesus, You took the curse of sickness upon You when You went to the cross. You've redeemed me from every curse of the law. If You took the curse, You took the effects of the curse. Sickness is an effect of the curse. I refuse to allow any curse in my body. I eradicate any form of sickness in my body. Body, you are free of the curse. I *see* my body without any limitation. Body, you are thriving with the life of God. (See Galatians 3:13.)

God, You have not given me a spirit of fear, but of power, love, and a sound mind. I refuse to fear when my senses do not line up with Your Word. You love me, and Your perfect love casts out all fear. (See 2 Timothy 1:7; 1 John 4:18.)

I am the body of Christ; I am the temple where the Holy Spirit lives. Where the Holy Spirit is, there also is the supernatural, healing life of God. Holy Spirit, You are working mightily in me right now. I *see* Your life flowing in every tissue, every organ, and every cell. The life of God is infiltrating every member of my body. (See Ephesians 1:22–23; 2 Corinthians 6:16.)

I am a disciple of Jesus Christ. Jesus, You said for Your disciples to cast out demons and to lay hands on the sick and they would recover. As Your disciple I place my hands on my body, and I say to sickness, malfunction, and disease—you go in the name of Jesus. (See Mark 16:17–18.)

My physical body and my mouth will be used as a vehicle to touch and heal many people. You have prepared me with a strong, healthy body so that I may do Your will. (See Hebrews 10:5.)

I worship You, Father, and so I see every sickness and disease fleeing in terror from my presence. (See Exodus 23:25; Deuteronomy 7:15.)

I believe, Lord, that You are perfecting everything that concerns me. I trust You with all my heart. I'm not leaning on my own understanding; I'm not moved by my senses. I live by every Word that proceeds out of the mouth of God, for Your Word is life and health to all my body. (See Psalms 138:8; Proverbs 3:5–6; Matthew 4:4; Proverbs 4:22.)

I cast down every imagination that is contrary to healing flowing in my body. Thoughts, you line up with the Word of God; by the stripes of Jesus, you are healed. This promise is medicine to all my flesh. I see this healing scripture flowing as medicine to every part of my body. I refuse to doubt God—He never lies! He is faithful and is performing this healing word in my body right now. (See 2 Corinthians 10:5; 1 Peter 2:24.)

I believe right now Your Holy Spirit, healing power is moving in every part of my body. I see it by faith. I believe Your Word over everything in the sensory realm that would tell me differently. Your Word is truth. It is above every part of the sensory realm. Your Word will not return void without accomplishing what it has been sent to do. (See Mark 11:24; Isaiah 55:11.)

FOR EMOTIONAL HEALING

Father God, I know You love me. I am fearfully and wonderfully made. That's what You say about me. You knew me in my mother's womb and have ordained me for purpose. (See Psalms 139:13–14.)

I confess my sins before You, and I know You have forgiven me of every mistake I have made. I am the righteousness of God in Christ Jesus. (See 1 John 1:9; 2 Corinthians 5:21.)

I see myself hidden in Christ. I present all that He is, not all that I am. Father, I understand You don't see all the wrong in me; You see Your Son, for He is my Lord, and I am hidden in Him. (See John 16:23; Colossians 3:3.)

I choose to forgive anyone who has hurt me, intentionally or unintentionally. I know God has forgiven me, so I forgive others. I refuse to give the devil any place in my life. I will not be a puppet in the devil's hand by keeping any form of unforgiveness. (See Ephesians 4:27, 32.)

I choose not to look back. Instead, I do what Your Word says: I forget what lies behind and press toward what is ahead, to be all You have called me to be. (See Philippians 3:13–14.)

I cast down every wild imagination that is contrary to what God says about me. Every thought of self-loathing, inadequacy, insecurity, and failure, I cast you down. God loves me, and His perfect love casts out all fear. (See 2 Corinthians 10:5; 1 John 4:18.)

I don't fear any man. I don't fear anyone not accepting me, liking me, or needing me. The fear of man is a snare, but I trust in You, so I am safe. God, You are for me. You accept me, empower me, and love me. I see myself loved by You, God. (See Proverbs 29:25.)

I refuse to be intimidated today. God has not given me a spirit of fear, but of power, love, and a sound mind. I wholeheartedly believe that You, Jesus, are greater in me than anything that is in the world. I will not be trapped by any fear, in Jesus' name. (See 2 Timothy 1:7;1 John 4:4; Proverbs 29:25.)

FOR FINANCES

Father, I thank You that You have given me the ability to get wealth and You add no sorrow with it. You want me wealthy so that I can turn around and be a blessing to others. I see myself wealthy. (See Proverbs 10:22.)

Father, I tithe consistently so that I am entitled to Your abundant provision. According to Your Word, I rebuke the devourer from my finances. I rebuke the devourer from touching anything that belongs to me. I declare that my family's material possessions (such as home appliances, car, and computers) last long. You are opening up the windows of heaven and pouring out blessings. (See Malachi 3:10–11.)

I honor the Lord with my wealth, with the first fruits of all I receive; therefore, my finances are overflowing. I see my checking account and savings overflowing. (See Proverbs 3:9–10.)

Lord, I believe You have provided me with financial seed to sow. I sow cheerfully and generously into the kingdom of God; therefore, I reap a generous harvest. God, You're making Your blessing abound to me according to Your grace; I am sufficiently supplied. You have made me rich in every way so that I can be generous on every occasion. (See 2 Corinthians 9:6–8, 10–11.)

Father, I am so grateful that Christ lives in me through the Holy Spirit. The Holy Spirit is giving me wisdom to find out knowledge of witty inventions. I hate all pride, evil, arrogance, and every evil way. Sound counsel and wisdom are mine. I love You, Lord, and I know You love me. I seek You early and find Your ways. I see those creative ideas. Riches and honor are mine in Jesus' name. (See Proverbs 8:12–14, 17–18.)

Lord, I believe You delight in prospering me. (See Psalms 35:27.)

Lord, I choose to obey Your Word; You said blessings will overtake me if I do, so I declare that I am blessed in all my "doings." You said You would order Your blessing on my finances and in my work place, so I believe both are blessed! I see them blessed.

You said You would lavish me with good things. I believe I am the lender, not the borrower; I am the head and not the tail. I am listening and diligently keeping Your Word. I refuse to swerve an inch from Your Word. (See Deuteronomy 28:1–14.)

I have diligent hands, and they bring wealth. Lord, You are enabling me by Your grace to leave an inheritance for my children's children. The wealth of unbelievers is laid up for me. (See Proverbs 10:4, 13:33.)

By Your divine power, Lord, You have given me everything I need for life and godliness through the knowledge of Christ. (See 2 Peter 1:3.)

Jesus, I thank You that You became poor on the cross, that through Your poverty I might become well supplied. (See 2 Corinthians 8:9.)

Jesus, You said You came to give me life and life more abundantly; therefore, I see myself abundantly supplied. You wish above all things that I prosper and be in health as my soul prospers. My soul is prospering with the Word of God, so I am blessed. (See John 10:10; 3 John 2.)

Money does not have me. I do not depend on it or my ability to make it. I fully depend on You, Lord, to supply all my needs according to Your riches in glory by Christ Jesus. (See Philippians 4:19.)

ABOUT THE AUTHOR

Tracy Boyd is the lead pastor at Grow Church in Naples, Florida, where people routinely experience the power of God through the Word of God.

Her passion for impacting lives for Jesus is evidenced in her more than twenty-five years of extensive ministry experience, which has established her as a visionary leader in the areas of discipleship, church planting, and church growth. She is known for her ability to teach the practical application of the Word of God in a way that generates dynamic results in today's generation of believers.

Tracy holds a Bachelor of Arts degree in communication from Oral Roberts University. She and her husband, Pastor James Boyd, are the parents of three adult daughters, who are quick to point out two of their mother's core beliefs: (1) our words have power, and (2) pasta should be eaten while it's hot.

NOTES